{

# FUNDAMENTALISM

/

/

/

/ CH46R1N 2019

}

-

```
{
      /
      /
      /
      / cum grano salis
}

-
```

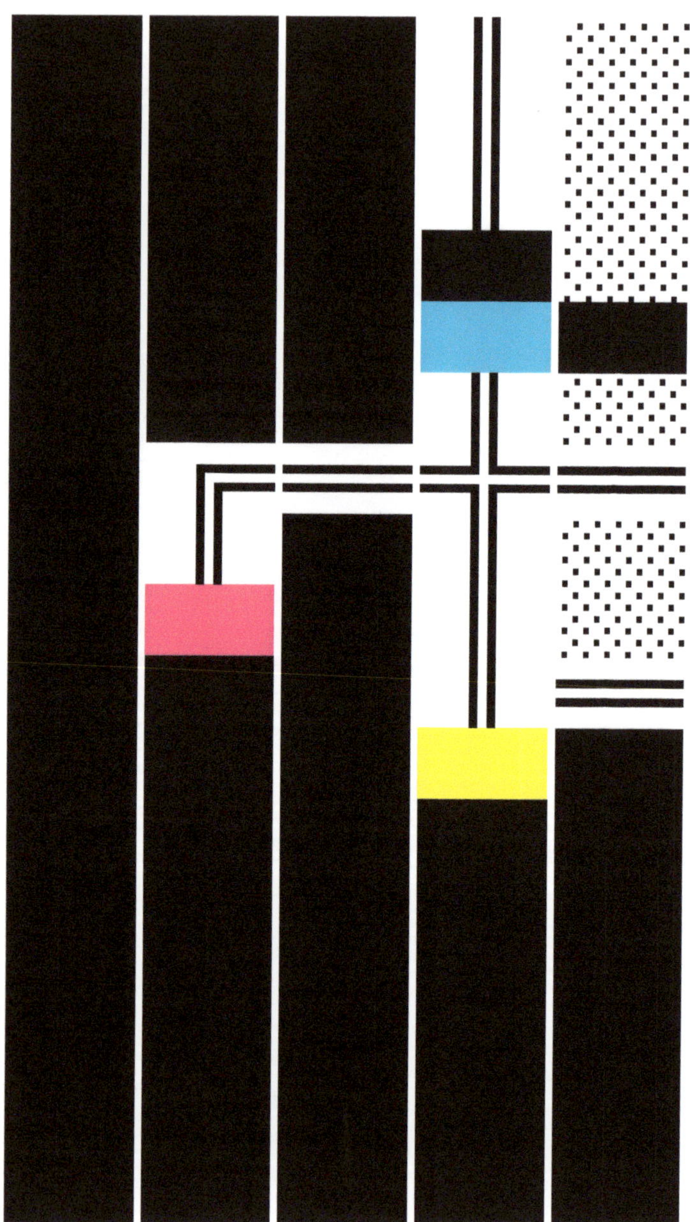

i.

{
 progressive loss of shame
     / ageing
}

–

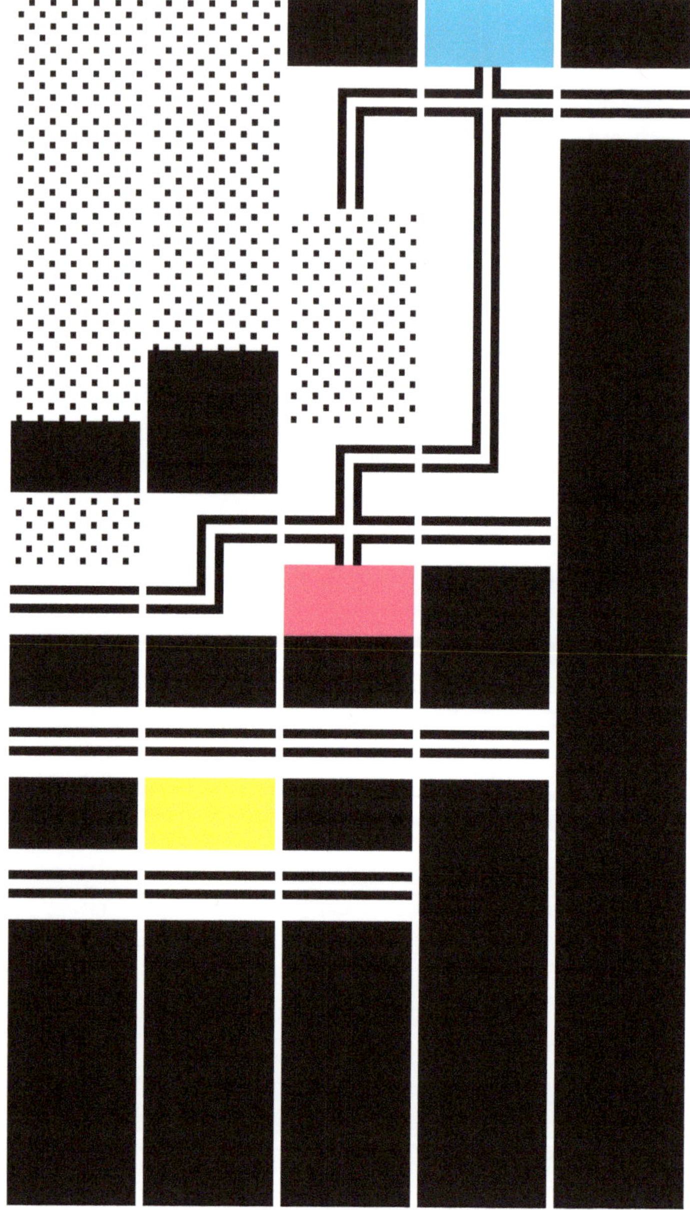

ii.

{
 powerful fiction
     / science
}

-

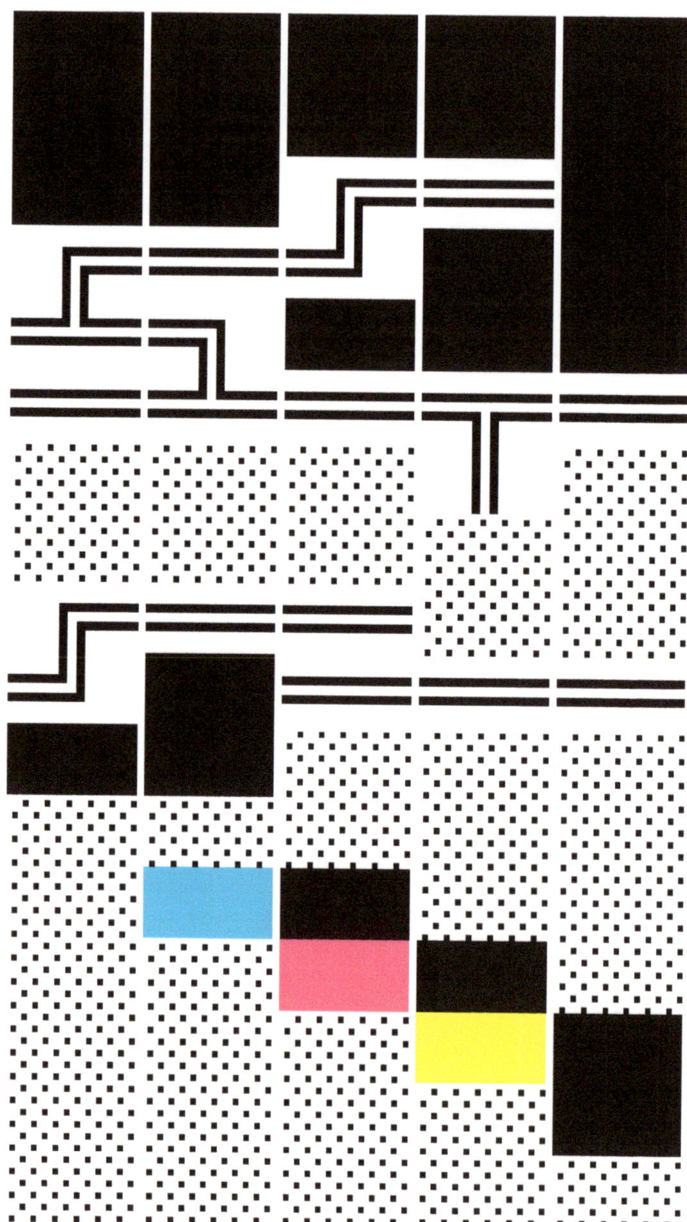

iii.

{
 fictions we choose to believe
     / reality
}

-

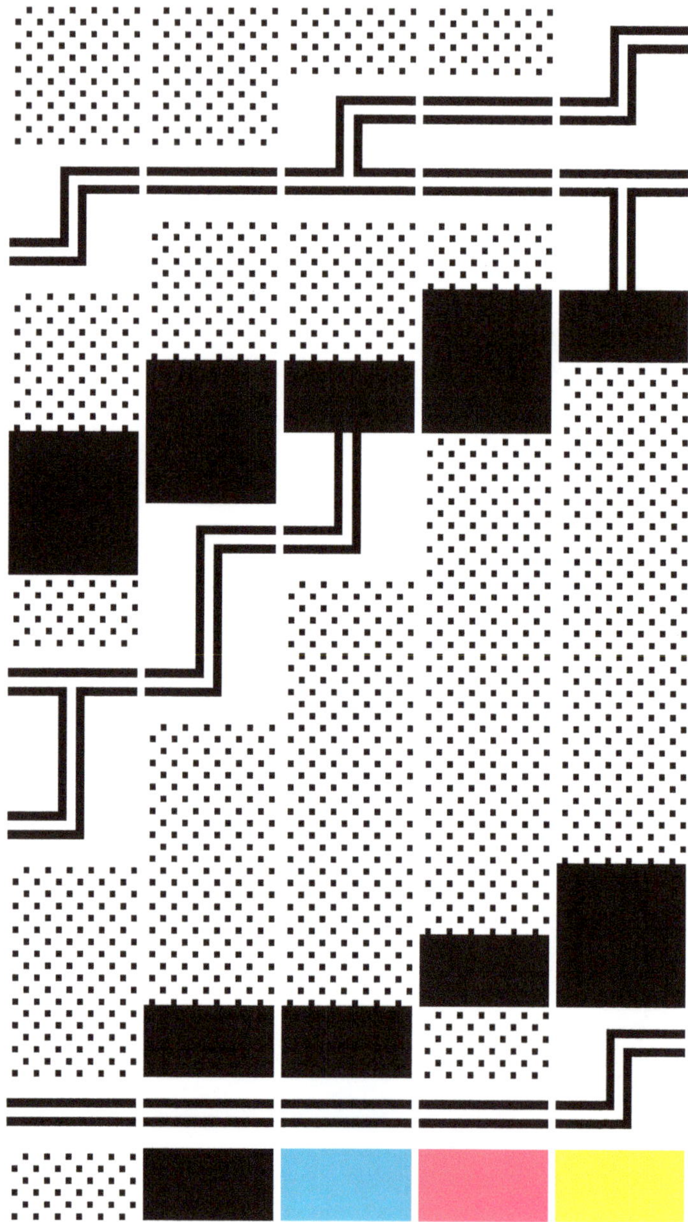

iv.

{
 buy cheap
     / buy twice
}

–

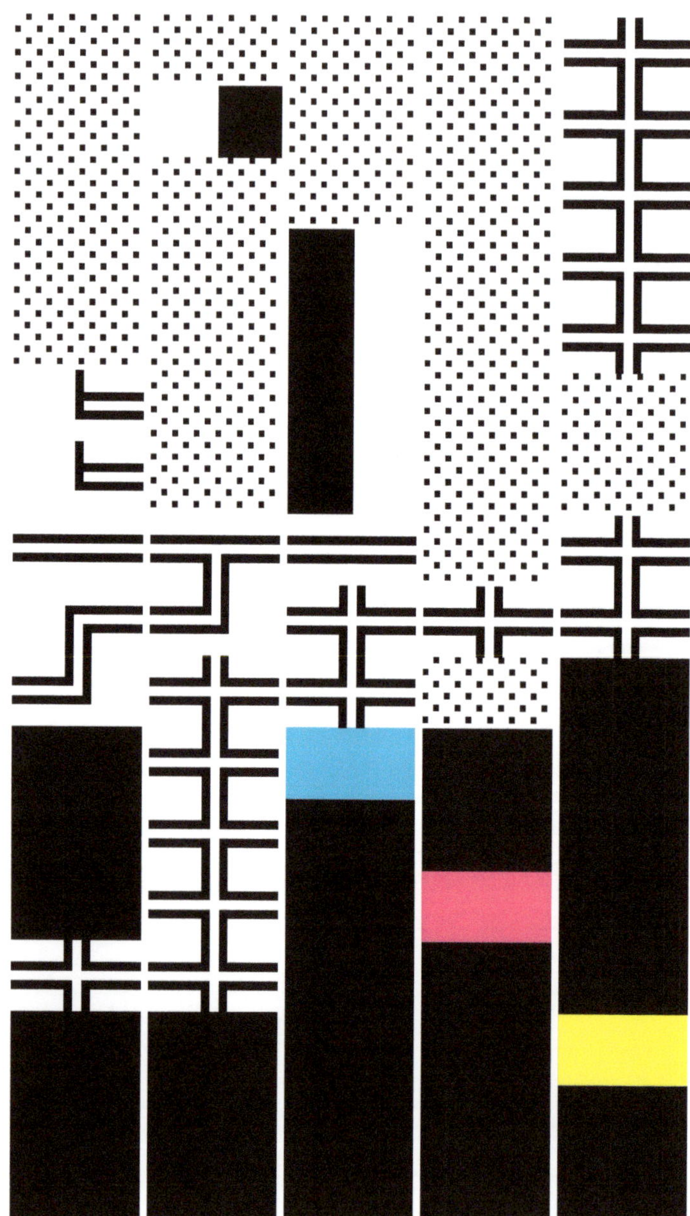

v.

{
 what spills over
     / share
}

-

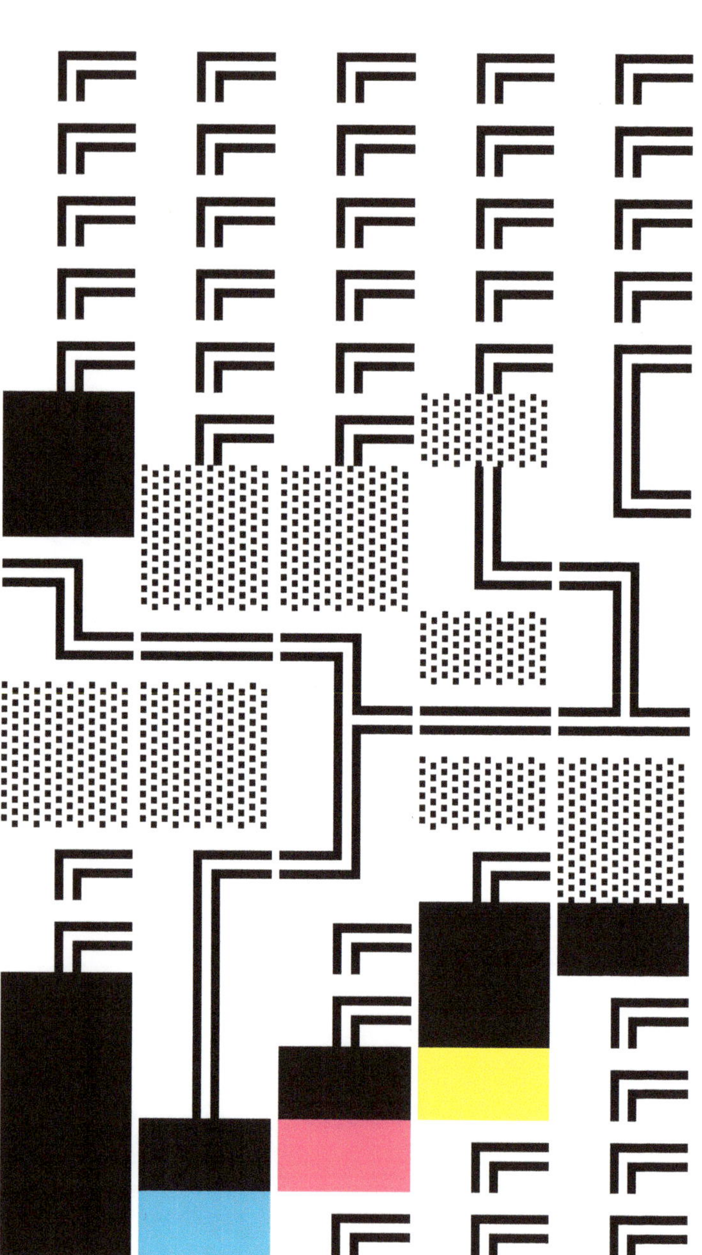

vi.

{
 from nowhere specific
     to nowhere in particular
}

-

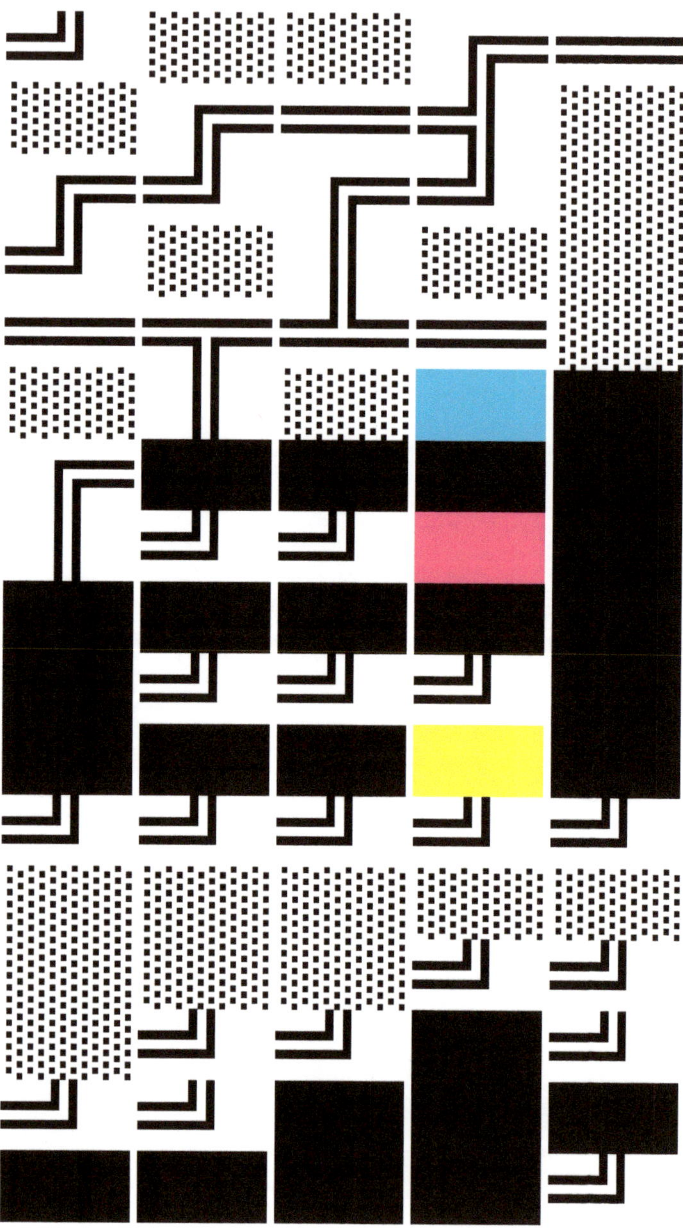

vii.

```
{
 be no one
      / act like someone
}

-
```

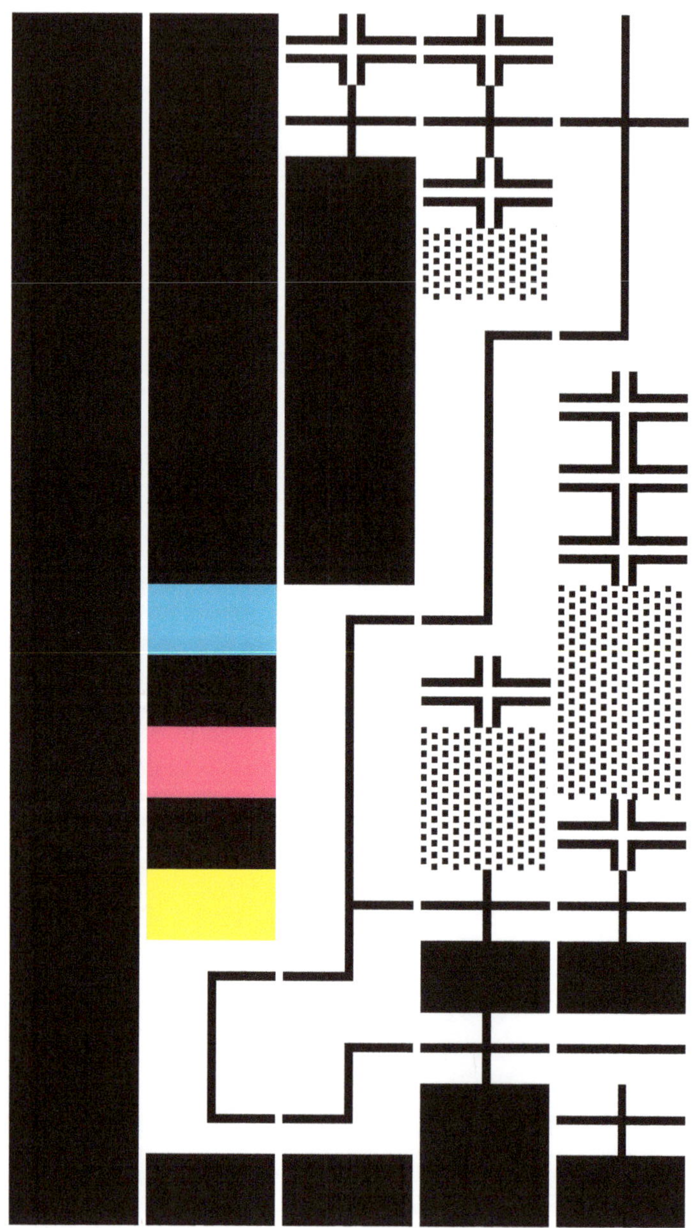

viii.

{
 when in love
        endlessness
                  when out of love
                            […]
}

-

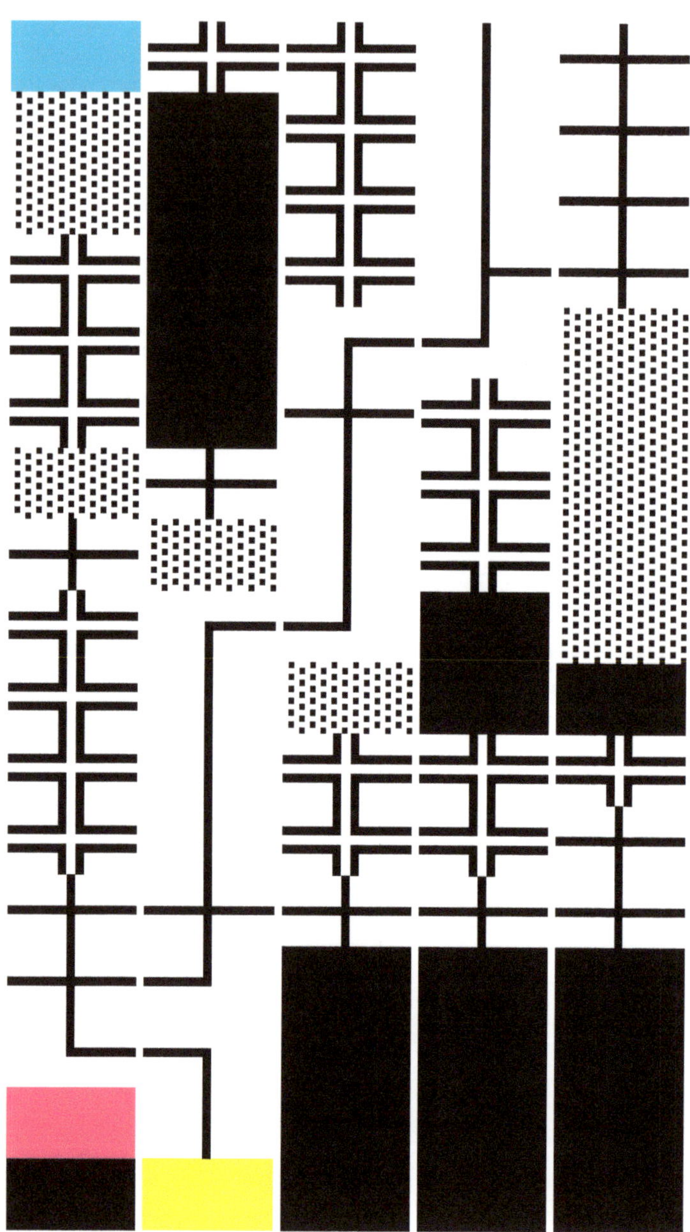

ix.

{
 oneiric surrender
     / not fear
}

–

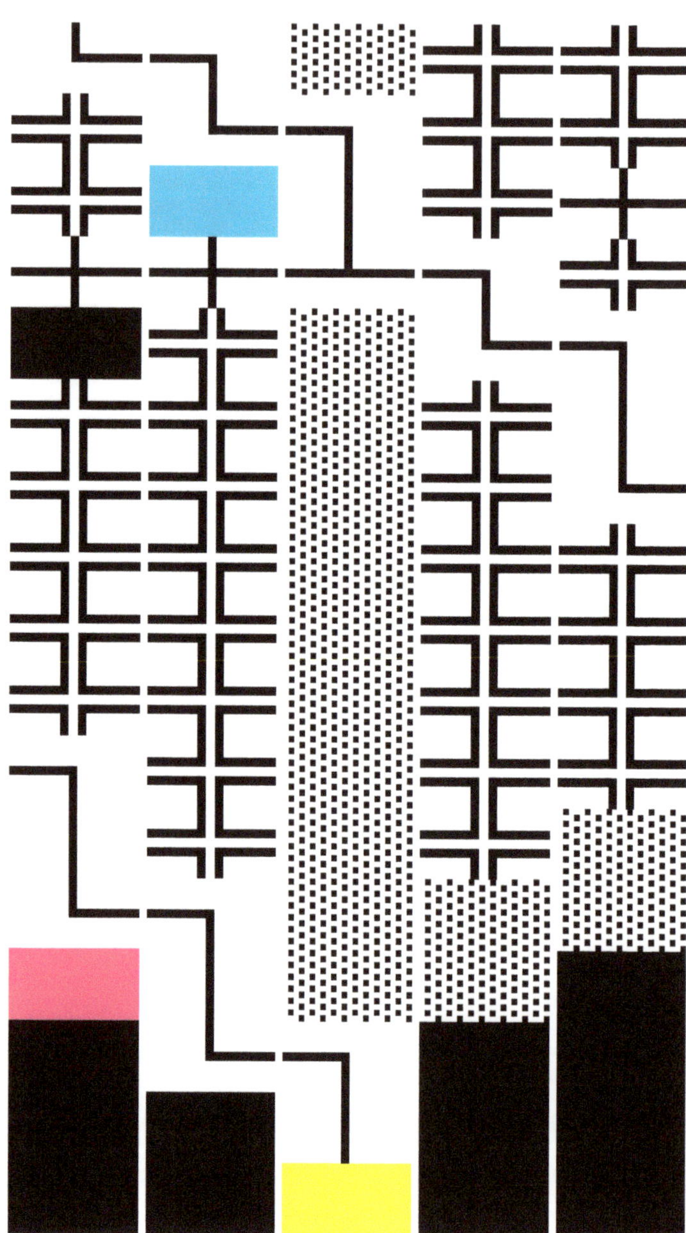

x.

{
 everyone has a tragedy
      inscribed on the body
}

-

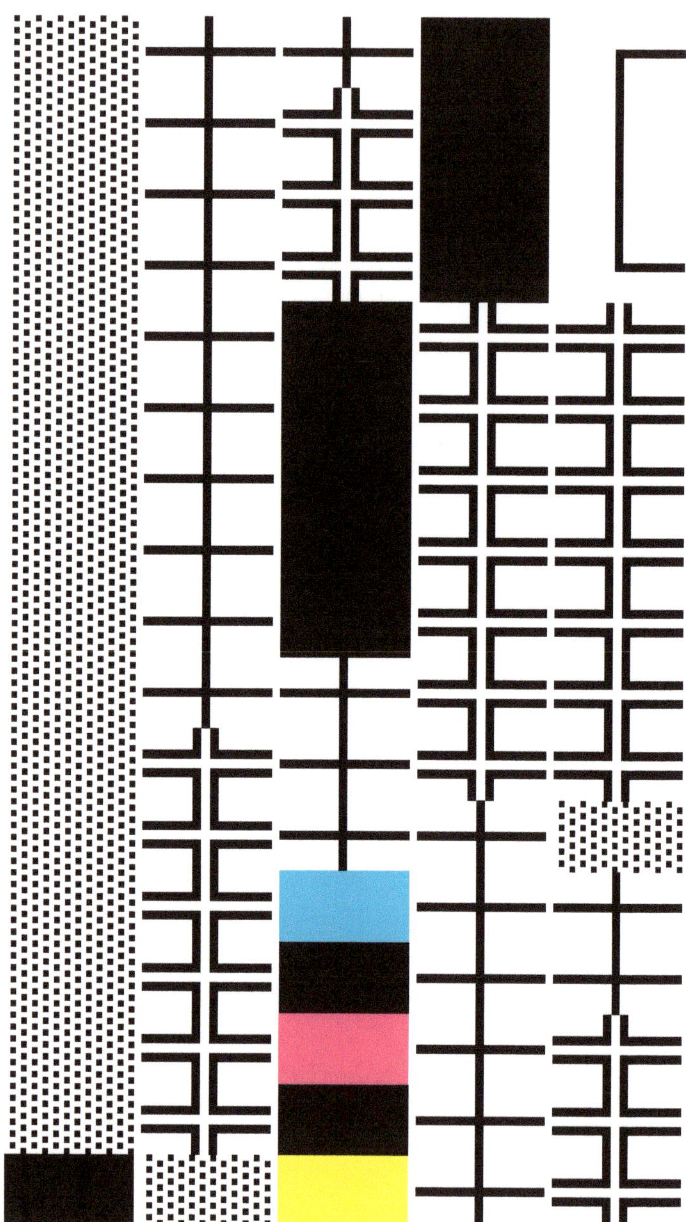

xi.

{
 we die
      / from living
}

-

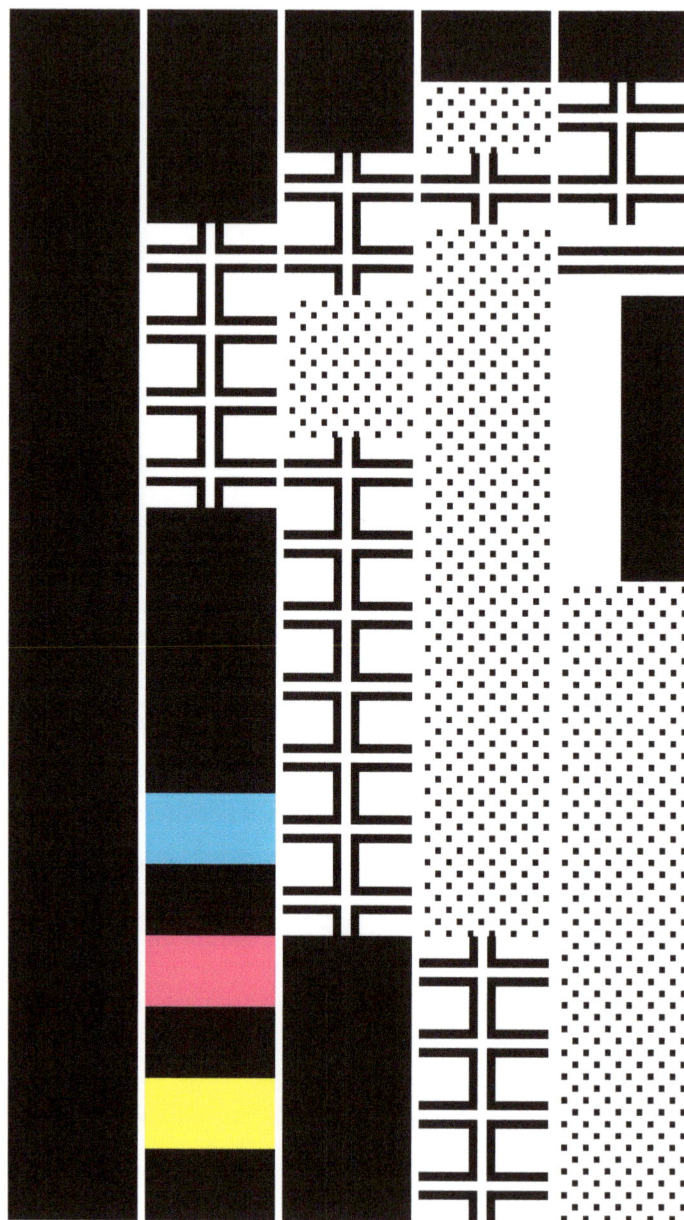

xii.

{
 being
      / not-being
}

–

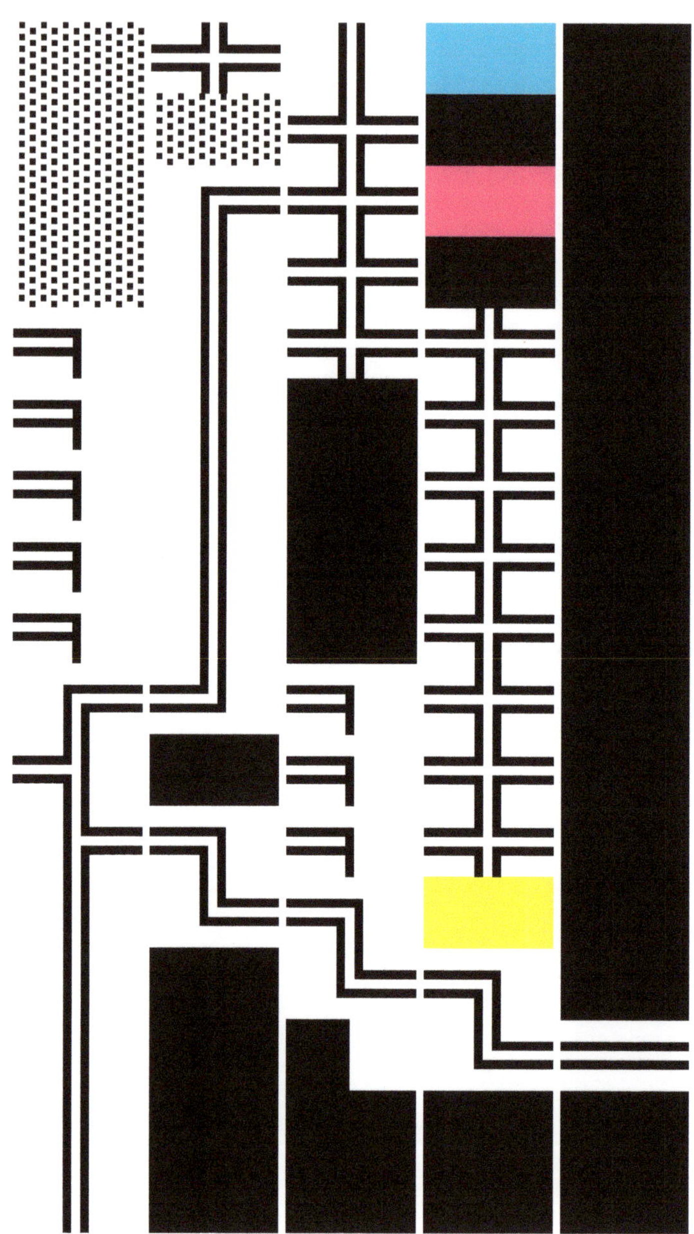

xiii.

{
sex
must have an edge of disdain
/ or mystery
/ or both
}

-

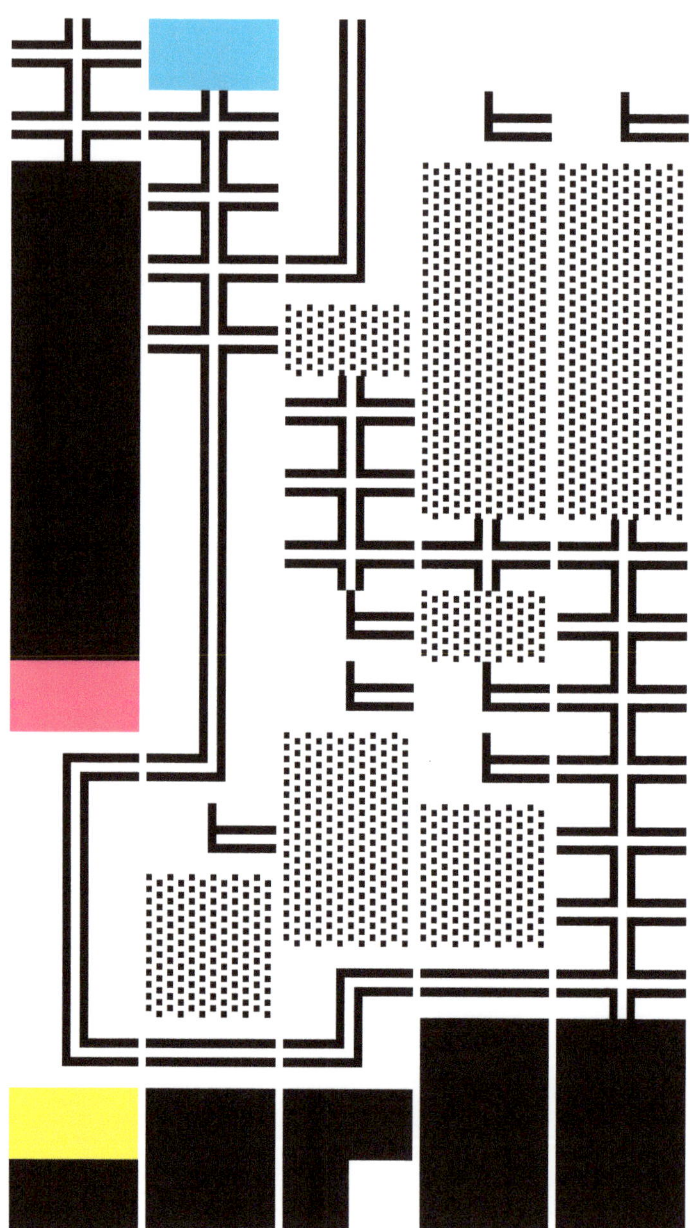

xiv.

{
 a complex set of things
     a multiplicity of bits
          / a swarm
          / a cloud
          / an i
          / not an i
}

–

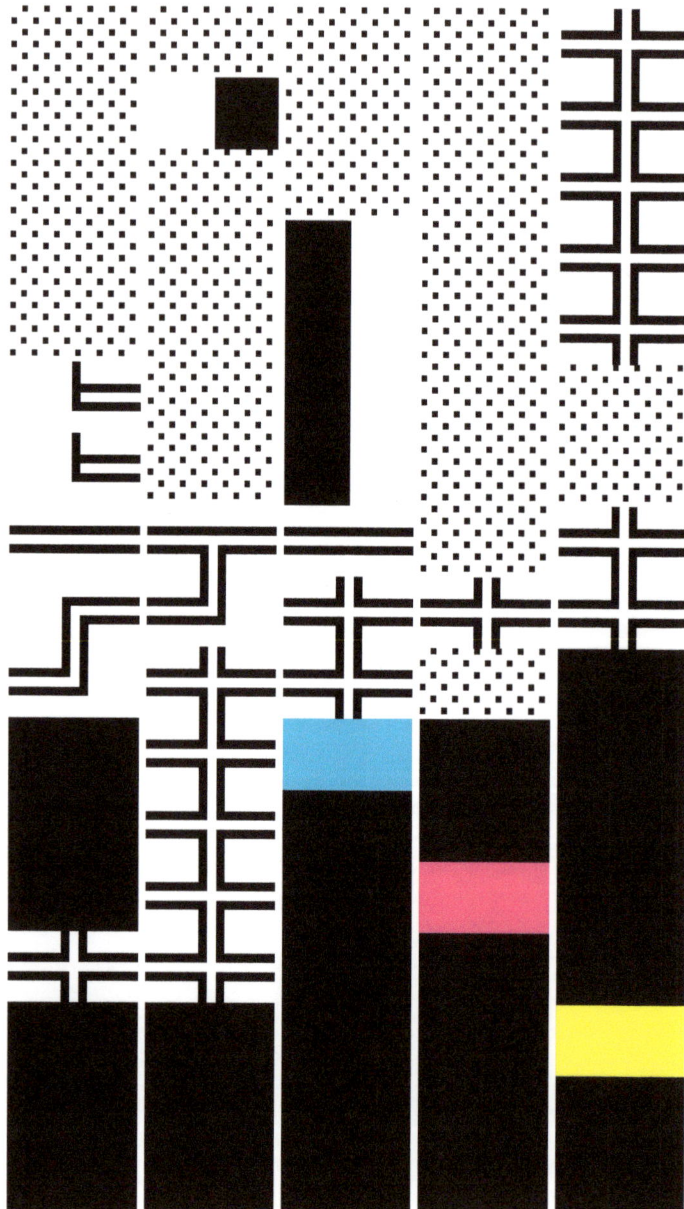

xv.

```
{
 build
      / tear down
      / self-sabotage
}
```

-

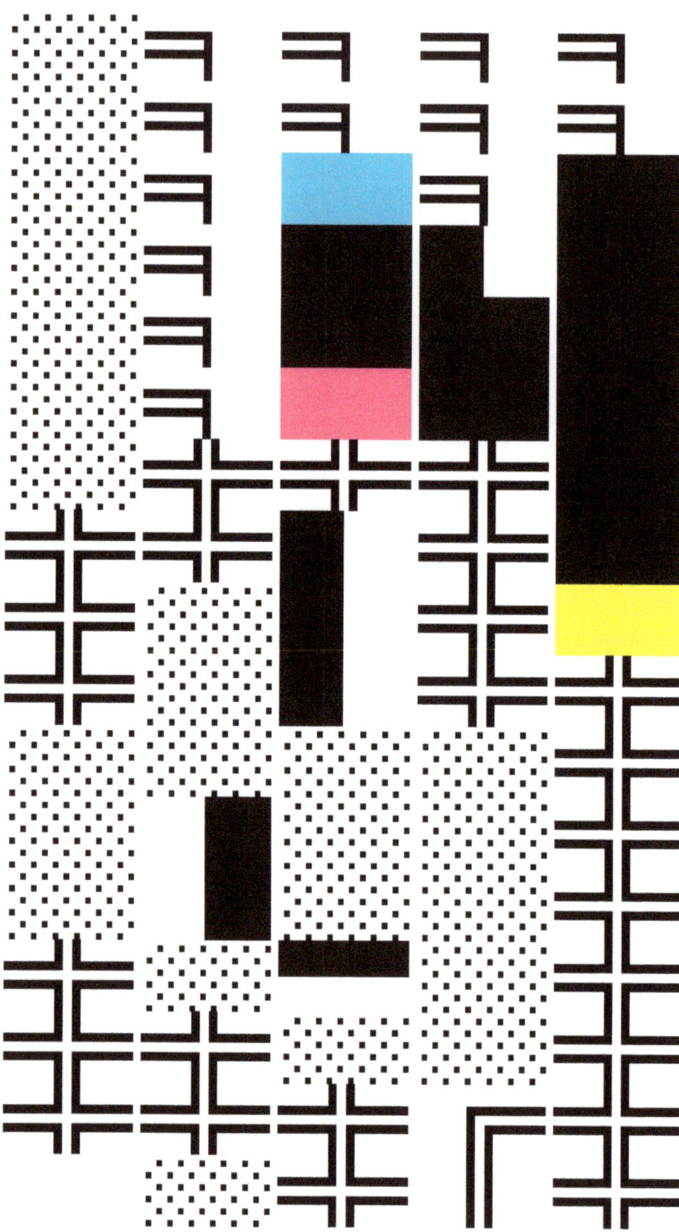

xvi.

{
after the end
conversations carry on
in the mind
}

-

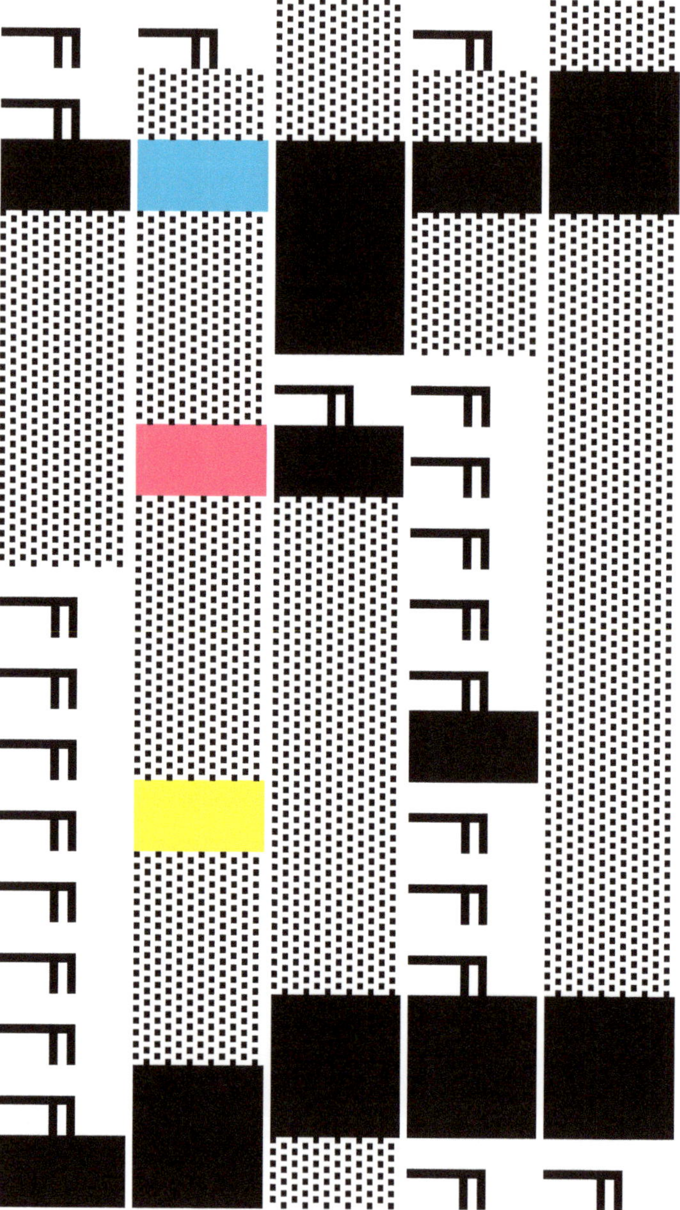

xvii.

{
 always falling in love
     / with ourselves
}

-

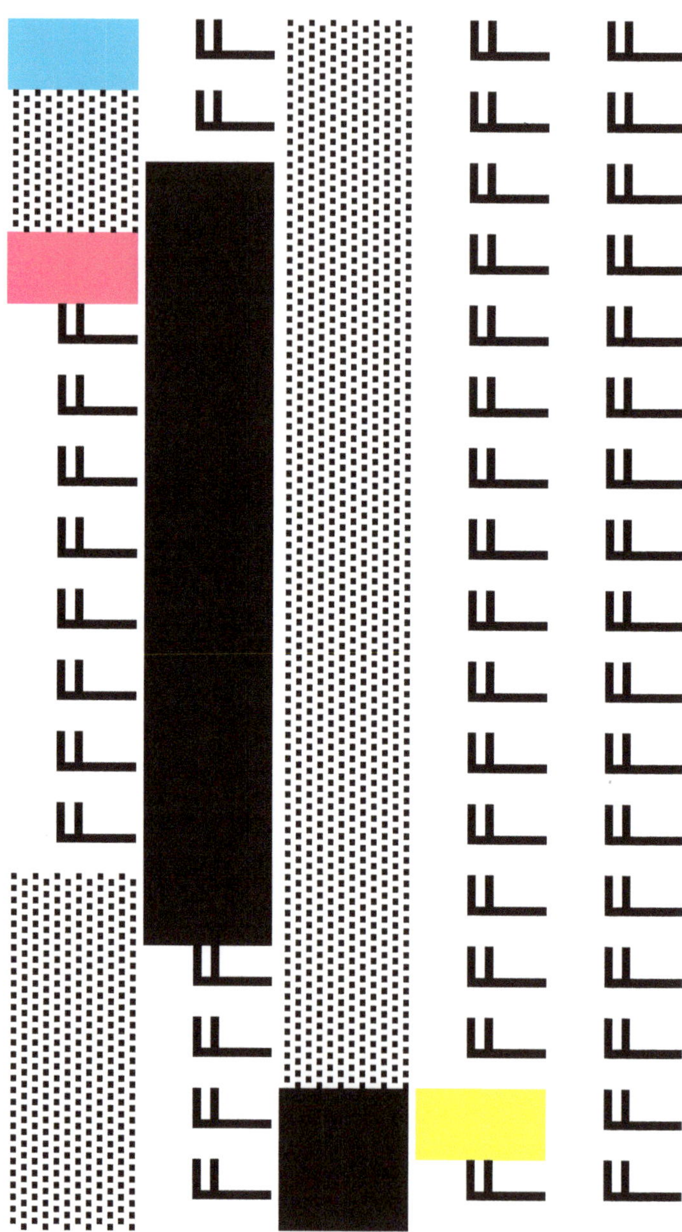

xviii.

{
 one who believes in freedom
     / best slave
}

–

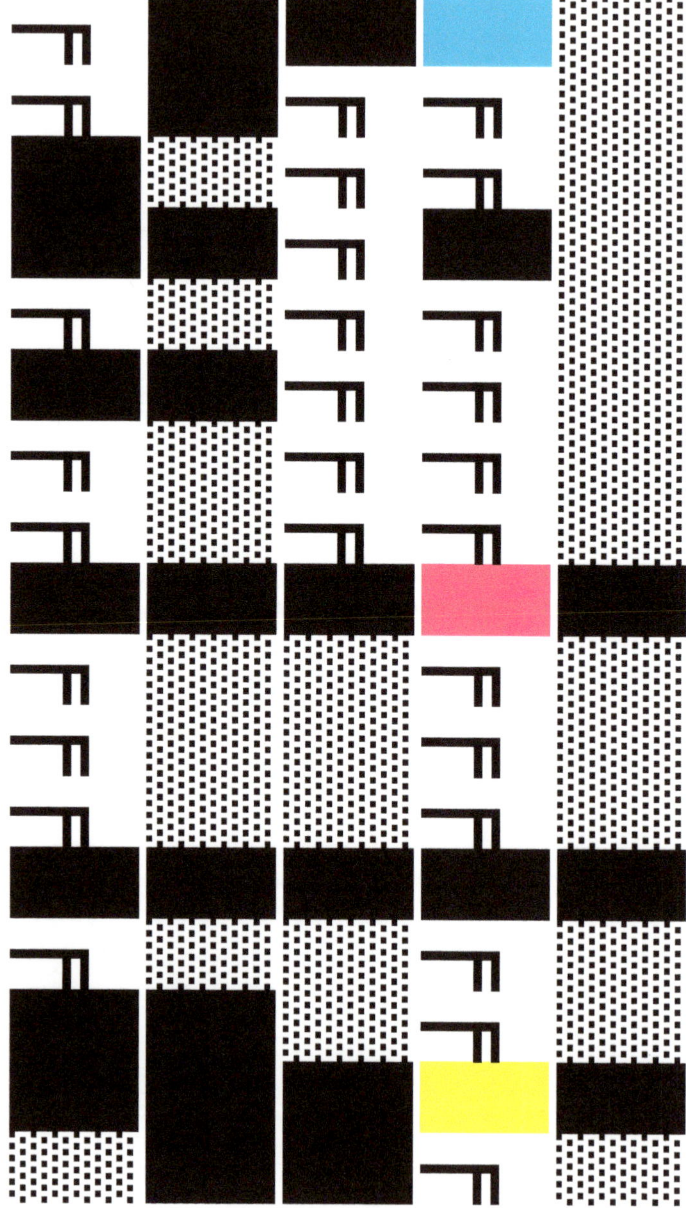

xix.

{
 to commit to another
     / highest act of freedom
}

-

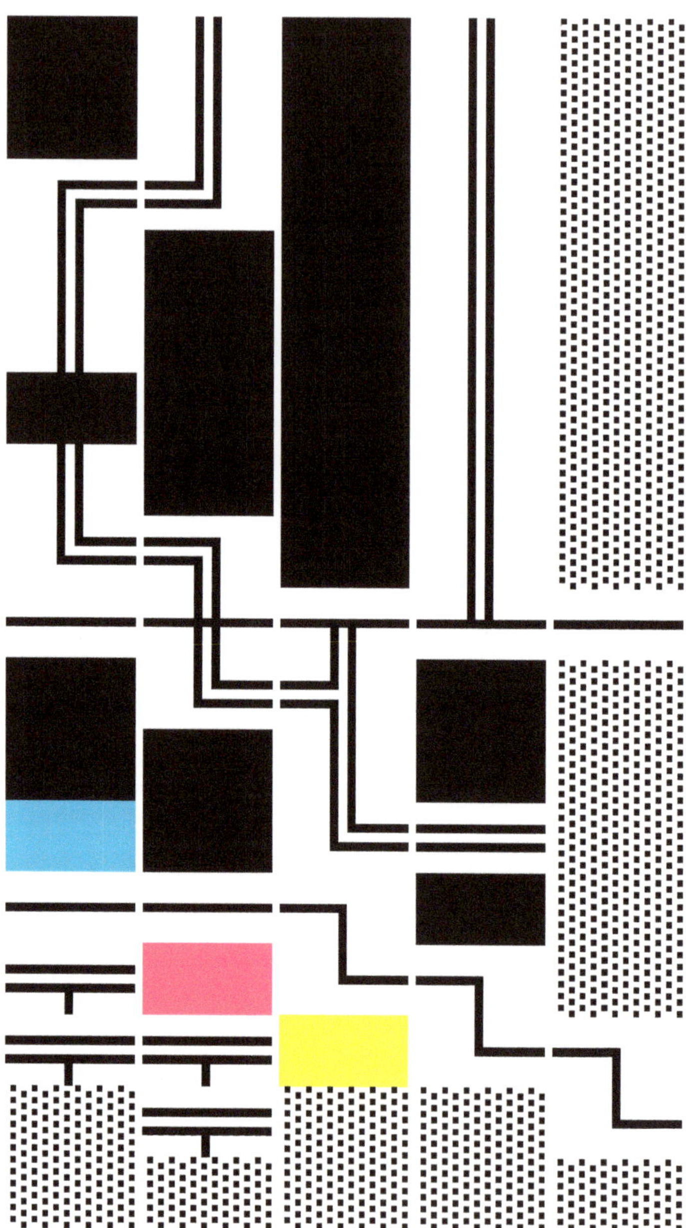

xx.

```
{
 set of things
     / body
}

-
```

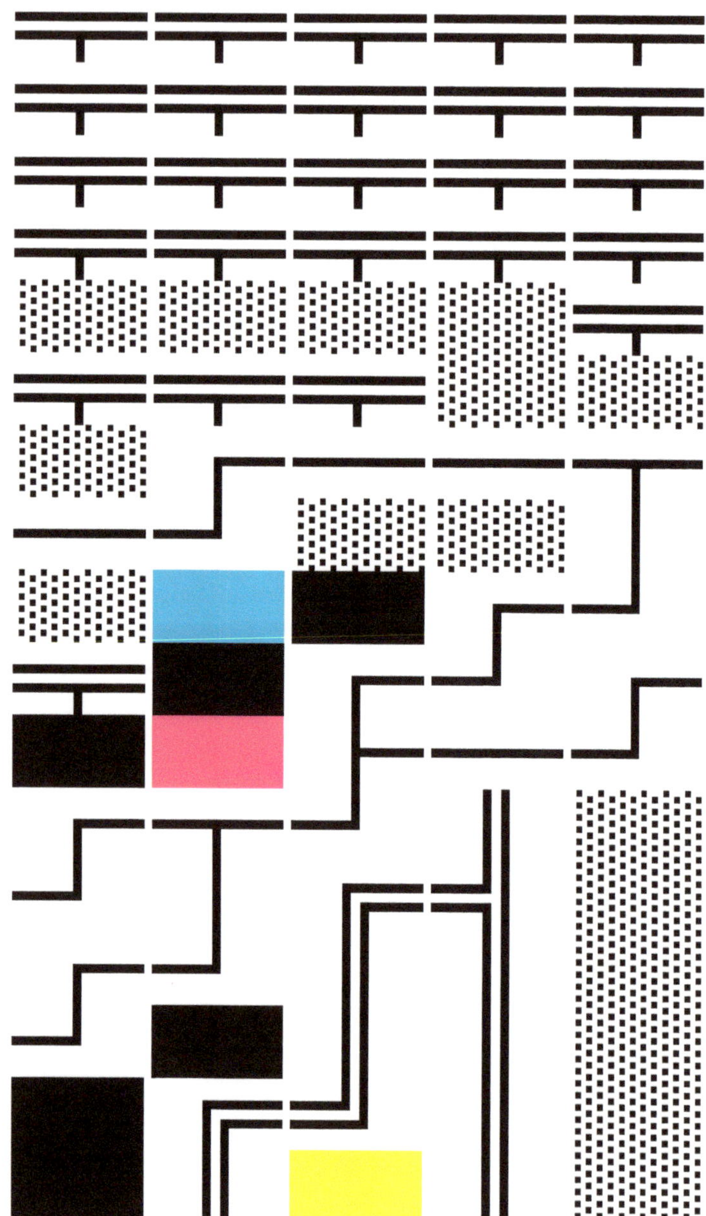

xxi.

```
{
 whatever
     / on
}

-
```

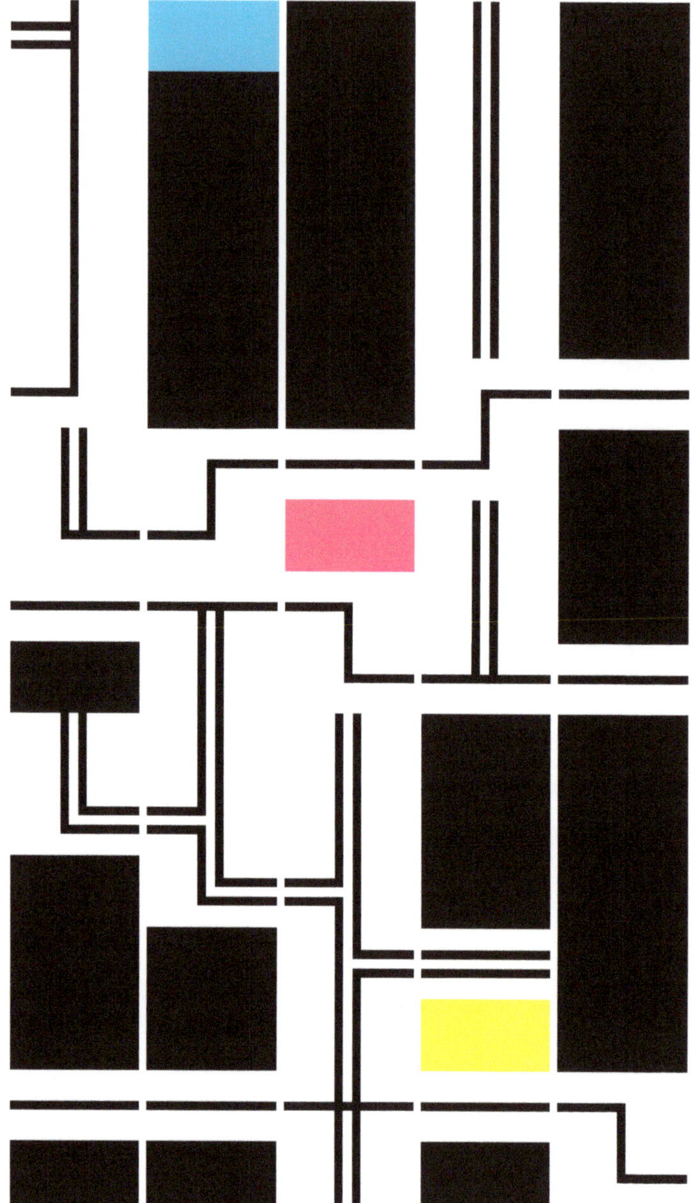

xxii.

```
{
 zero
     fucks
          given
}
```

-

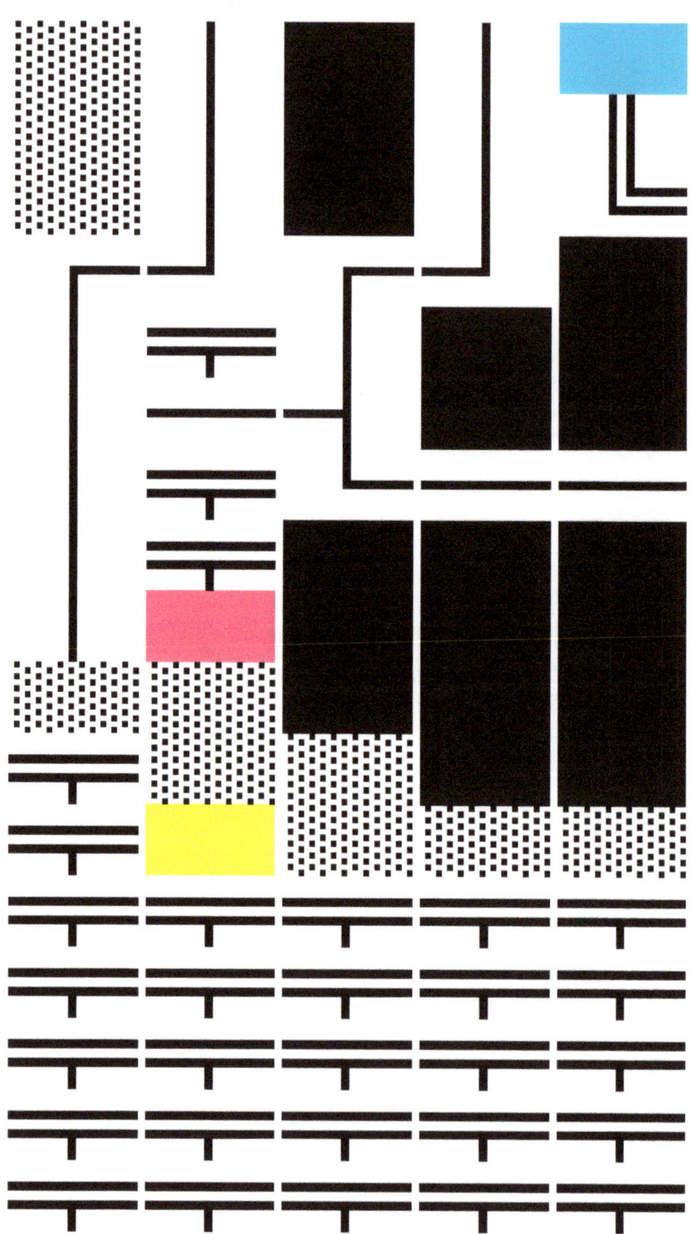

xxiii.

```
{
 life is ugly
     therein lies
           its beauty
}
```

-

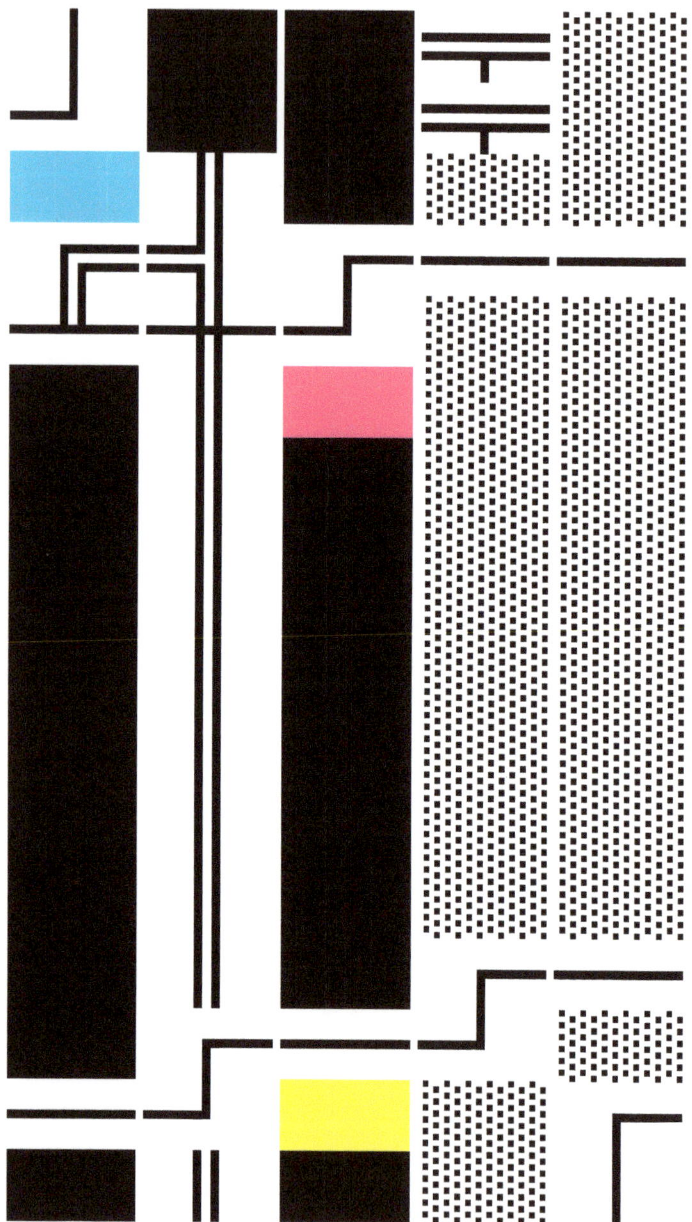

xxiv.

{
 definitely
     / maybe
}

–

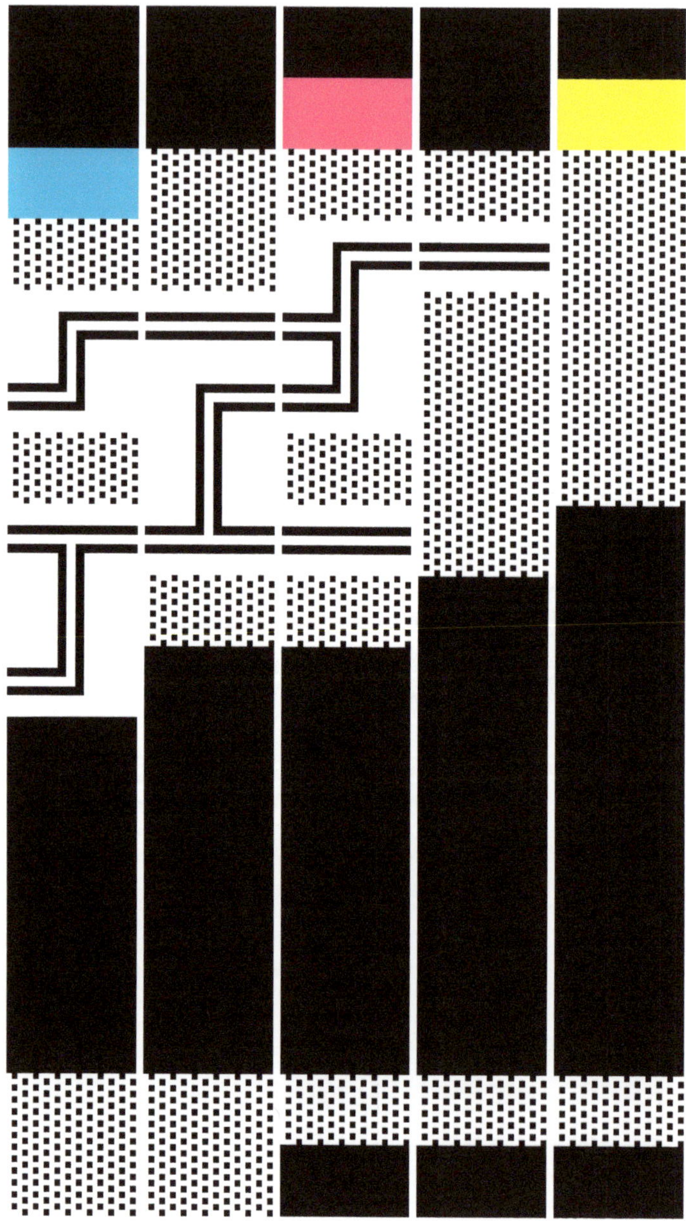

xxv.

```
{
 past
     / happened
 future
     / yet to happen
 present
     / neither
}
```

-

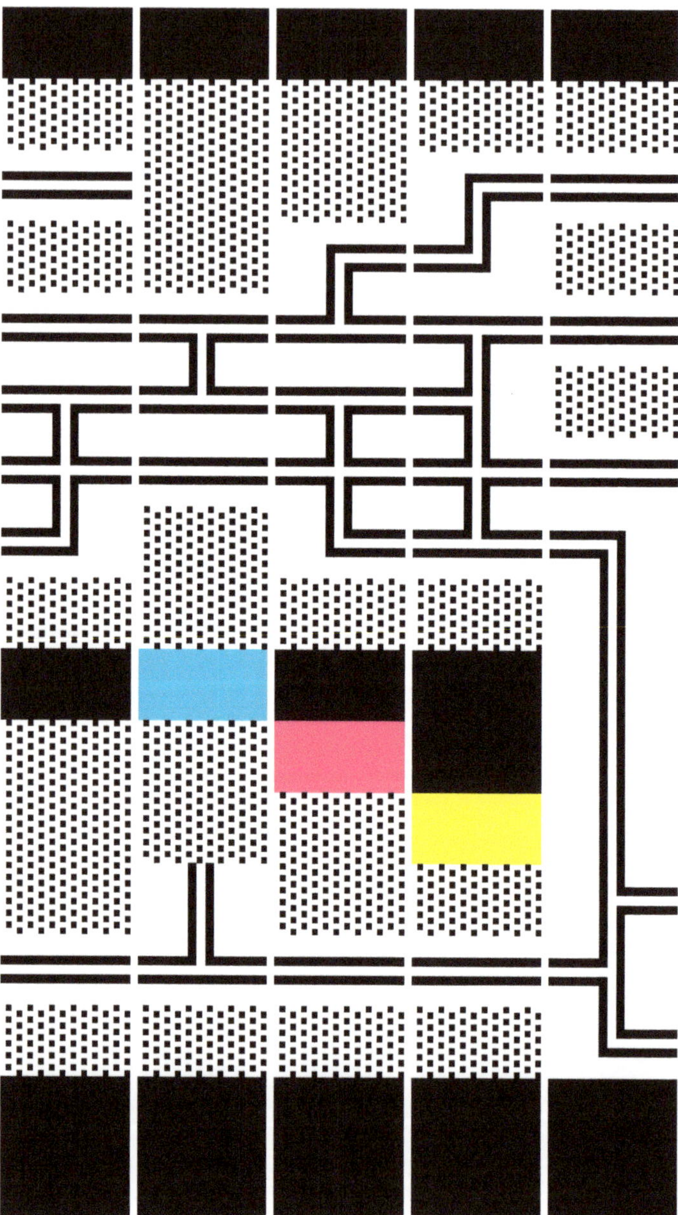

xxvi.

```
{
 make visible
     what is invisible
           see what happens
}
```

-

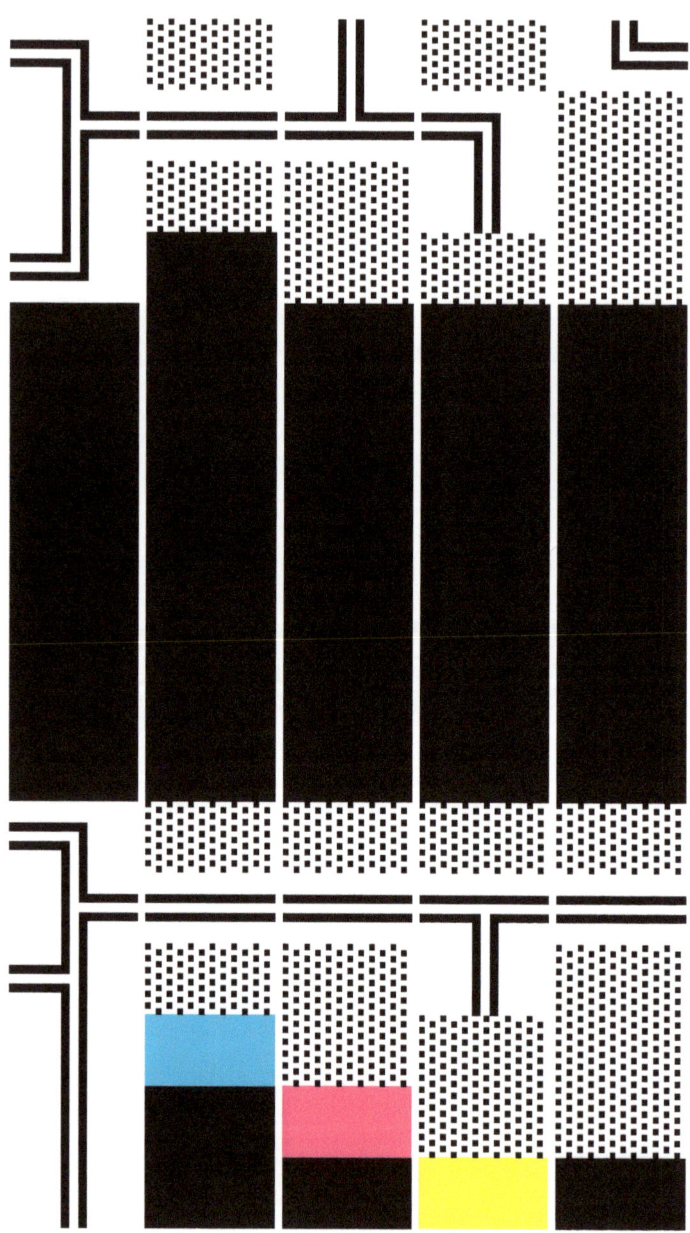

xxvii.

{
 pun
 / intended
}

-

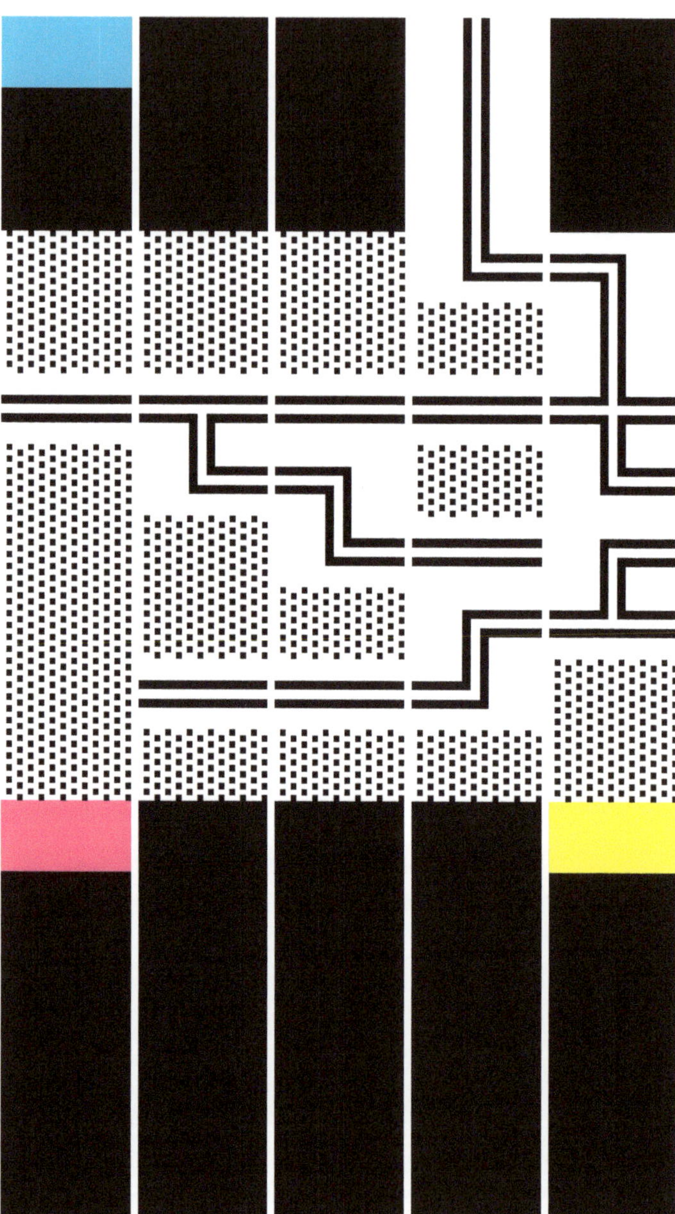

xxviii.

{
 superstition
      / brings bad luck
}

–

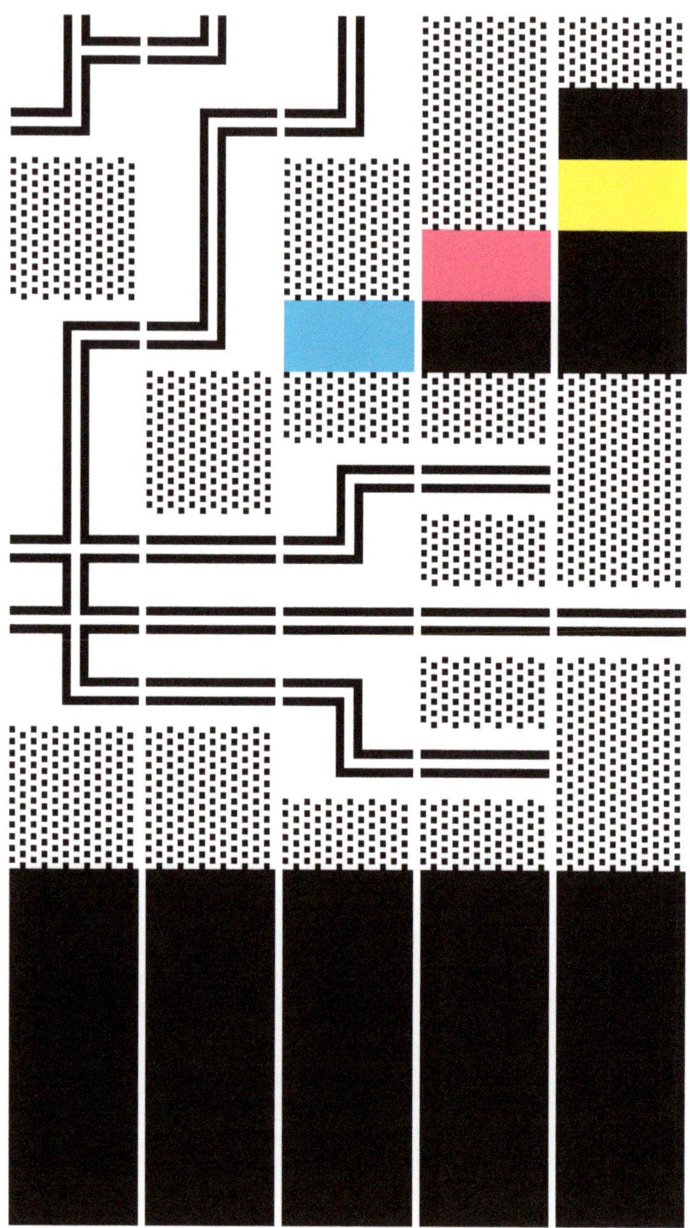

xxix.

{
 not photogenic
     / photohygienic
}

-

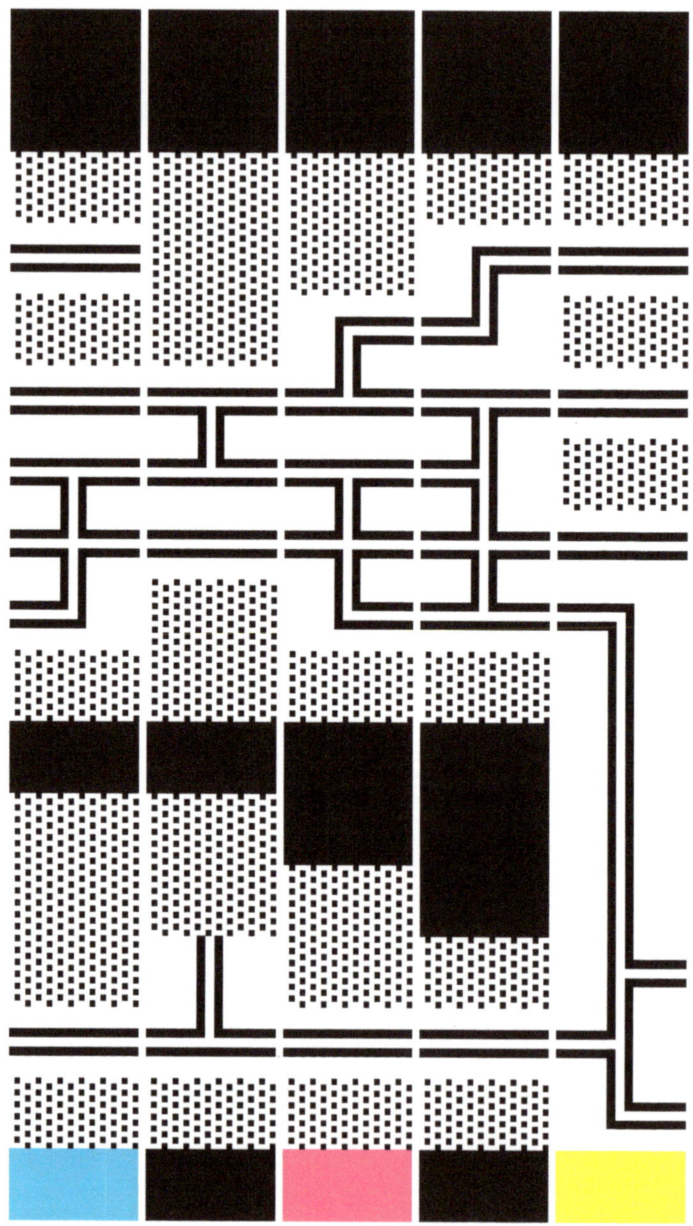

xxx.

{
 low-res
     / love-mode
}

–

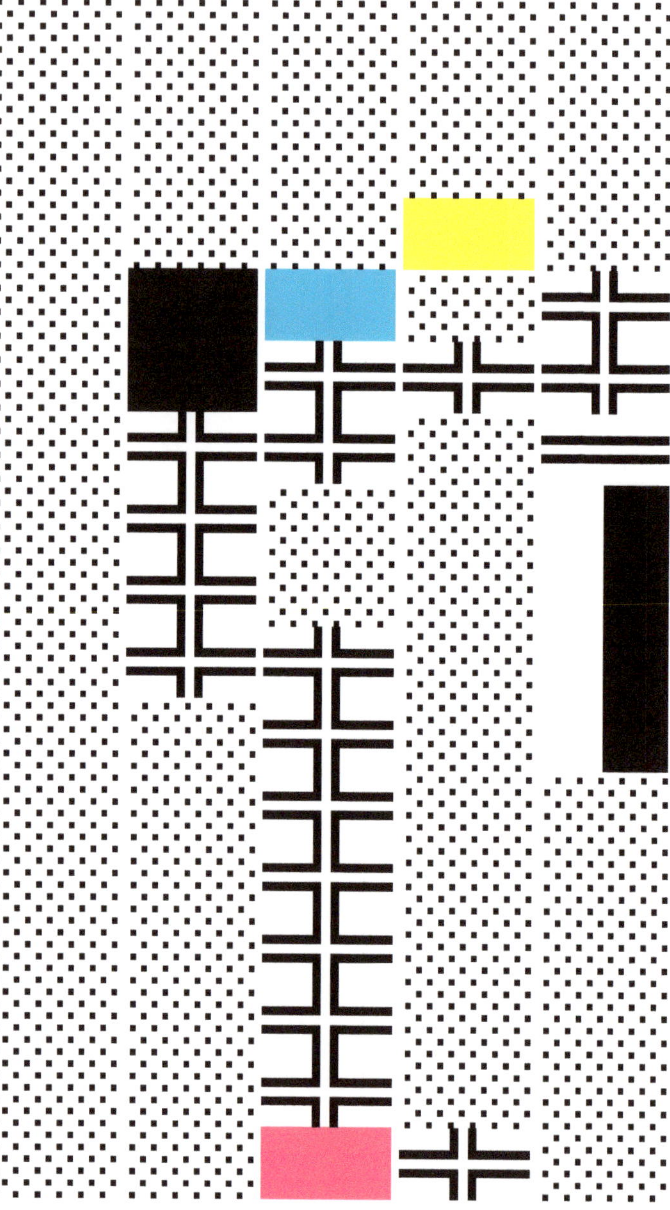

xxxi.

```
{
 yeah
     right
          whatever
}
```

-

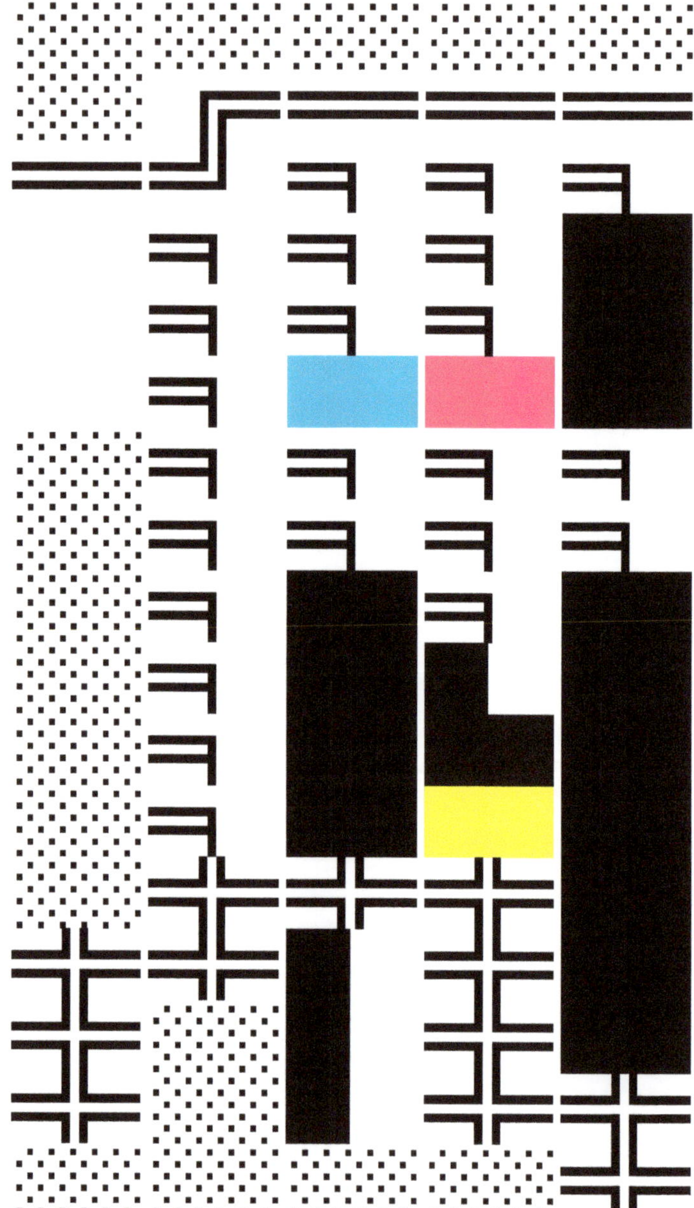

xxxii.

{
 post-everything
     / neo-nothing
}

-

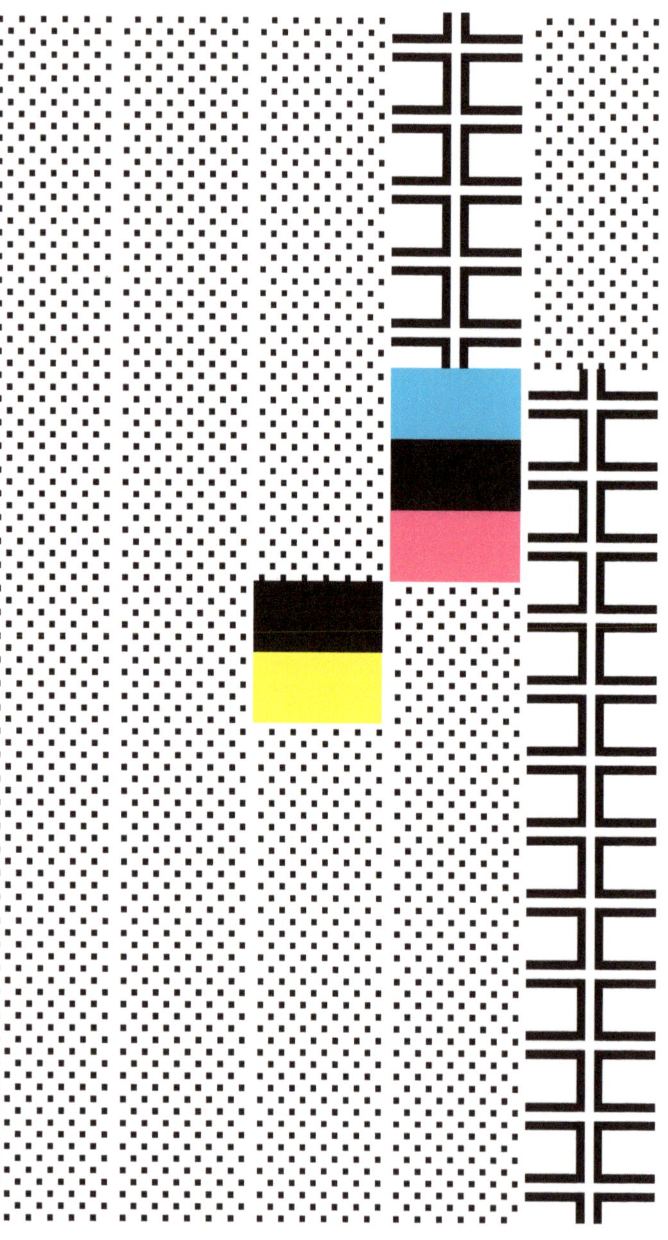

xxxiii.

{
 what we wished for
     / hell
}

-

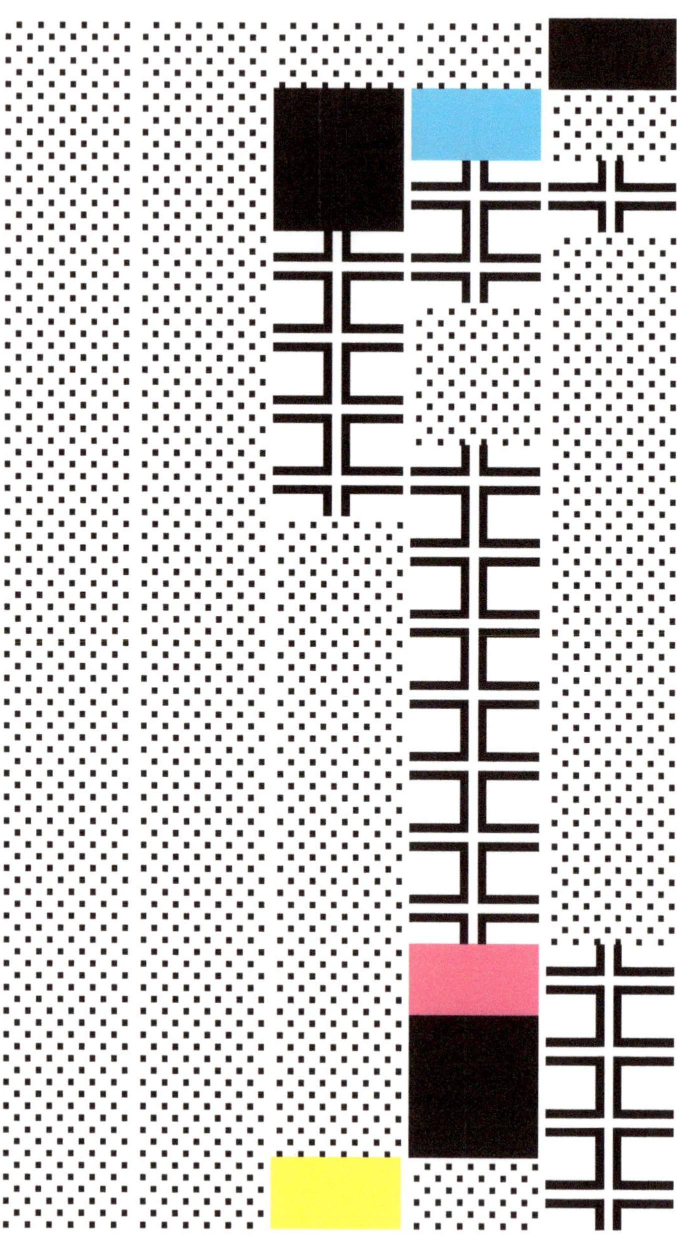

xxxiv.

{
 mesh of random phenomena
     / life
}

-

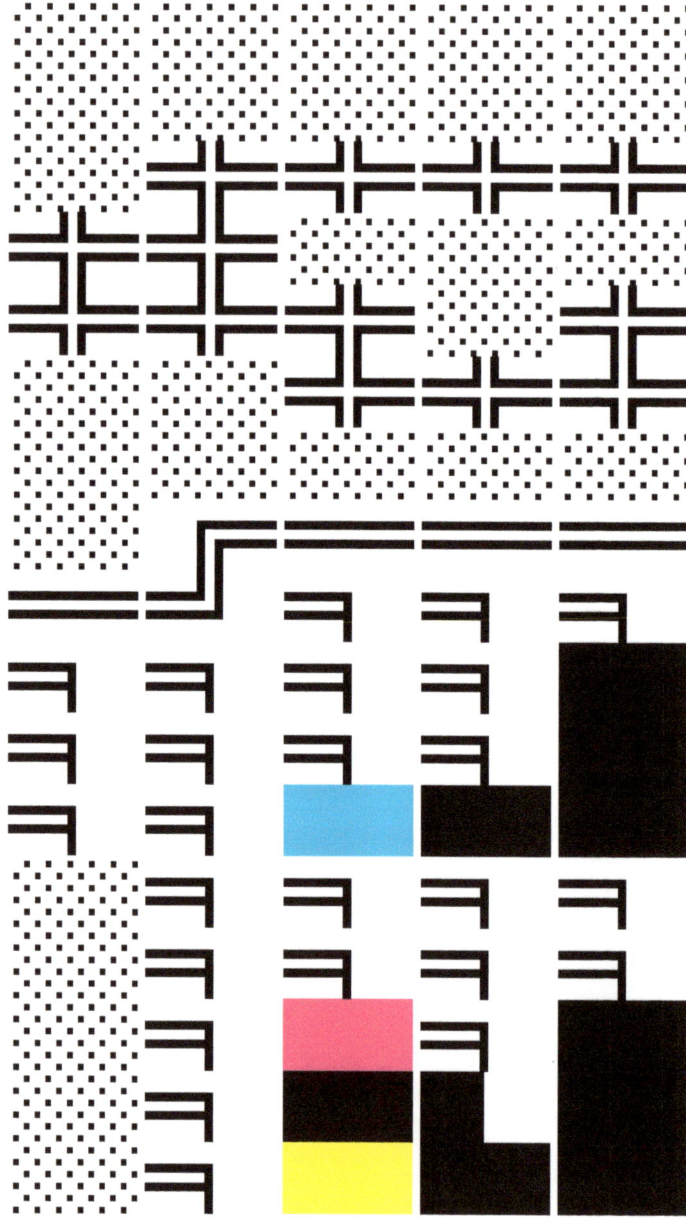

xxxv.

{
we don't know what we want
but we know we want something
}

-

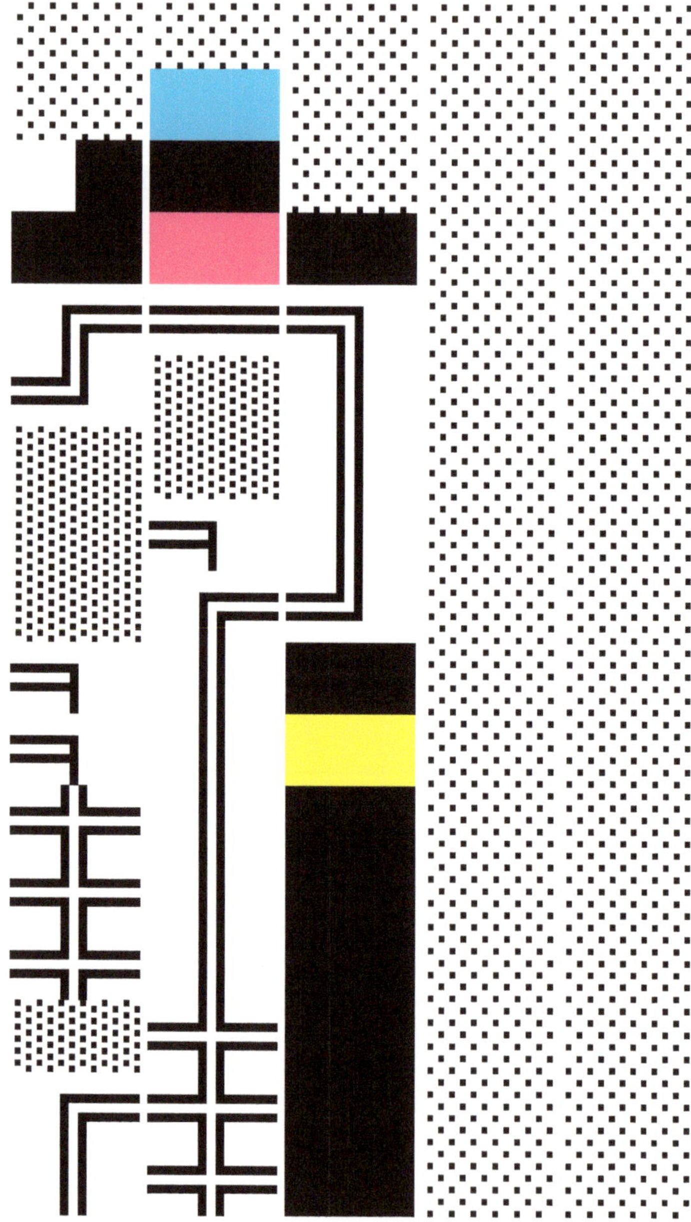

xxxvi.

{
measure of frustration
/ equivalent
/ to measure of desire
}

–

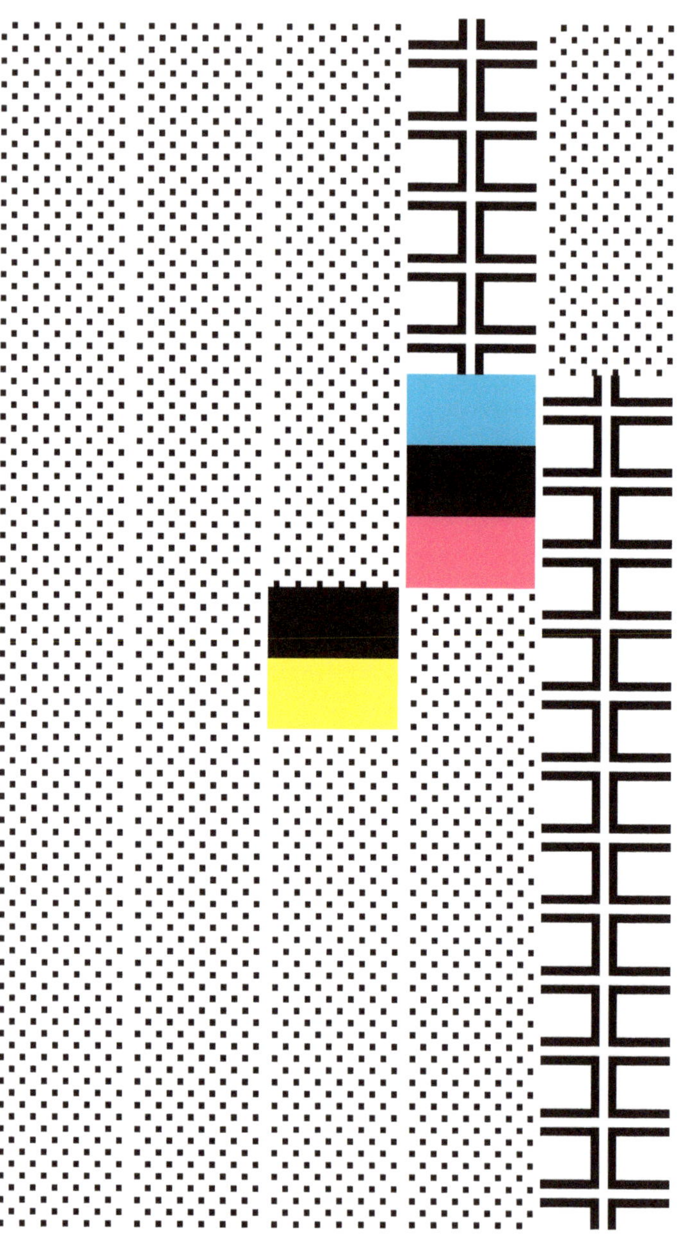

xxxvii.

{
 entertaining ourselves
     / to death
}

-

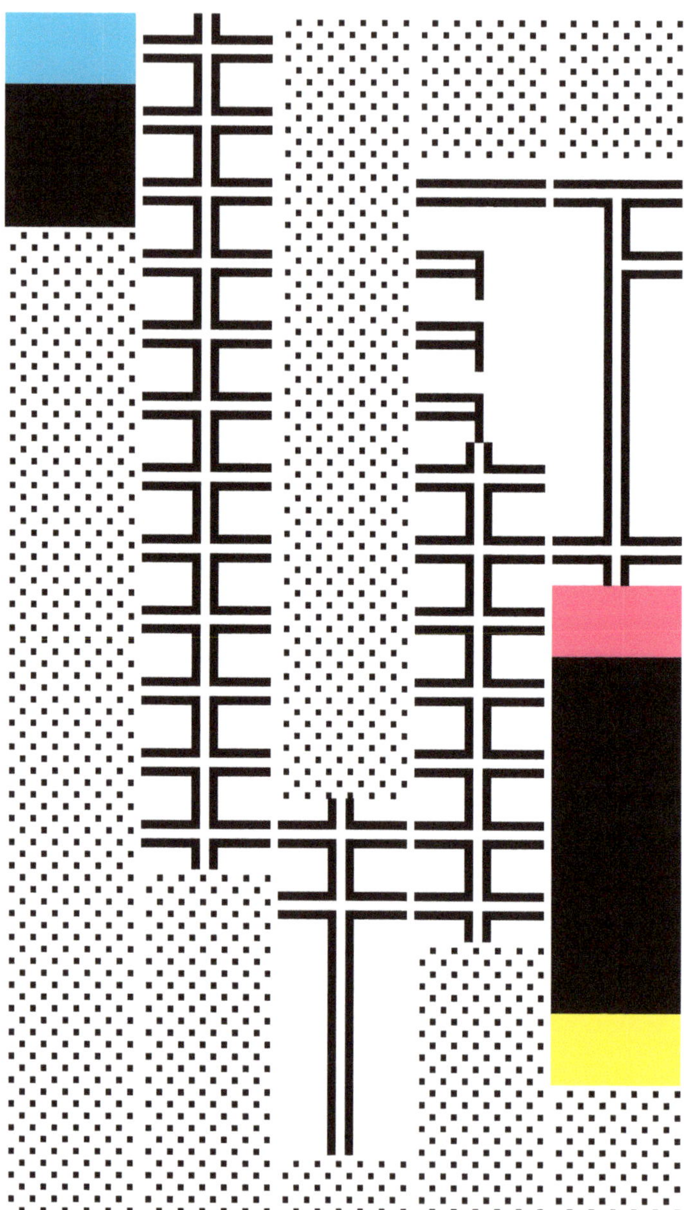

xxxviii.

```
{
 de-program
      / goodness
      / beauty
      / truth
}
```

-

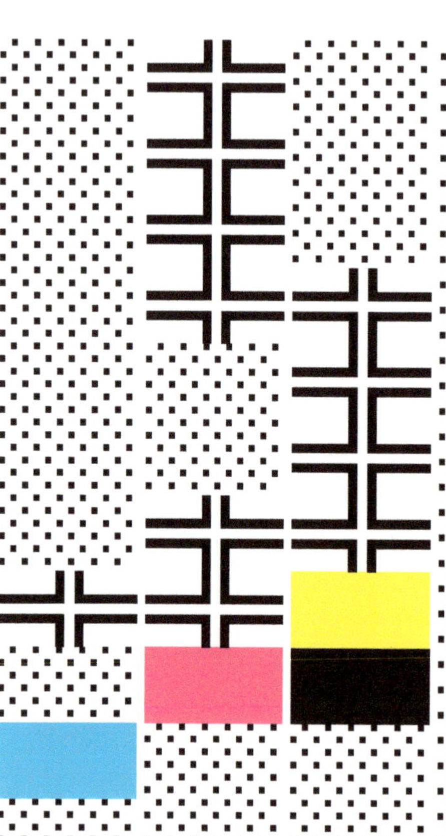

xxxix.

{
 cultivate
     relations
}

-

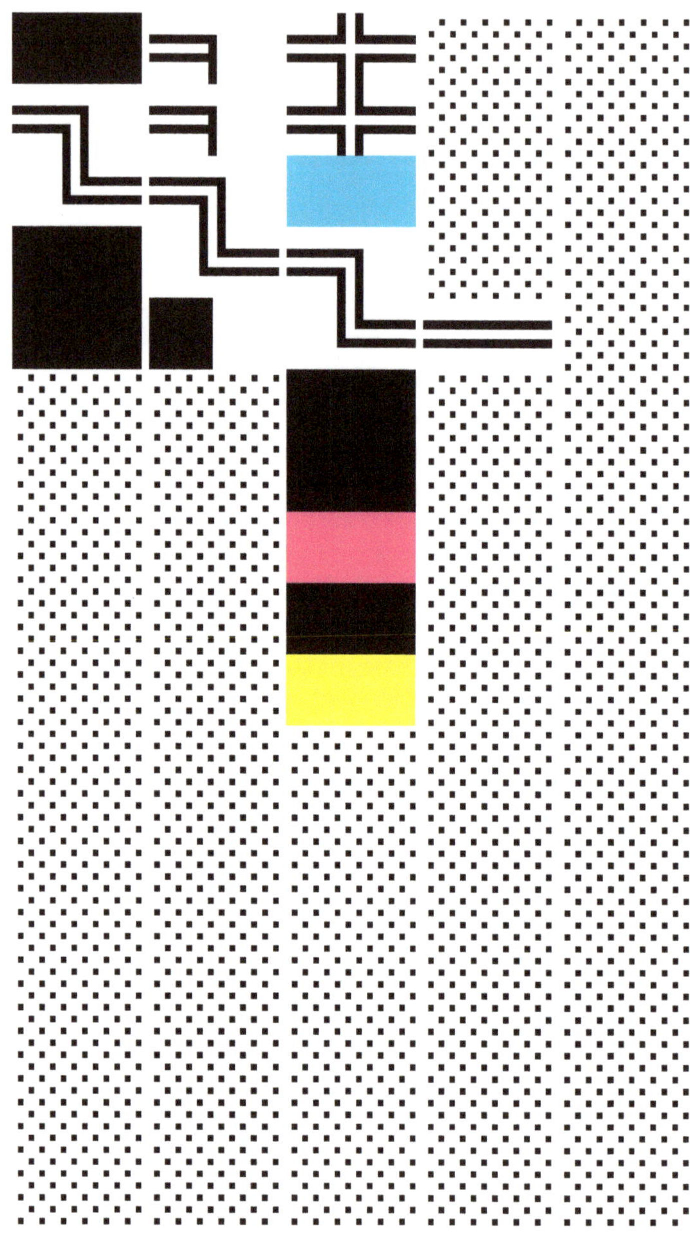

xl.

{
 mutual penetration
     / dialogue
}

–

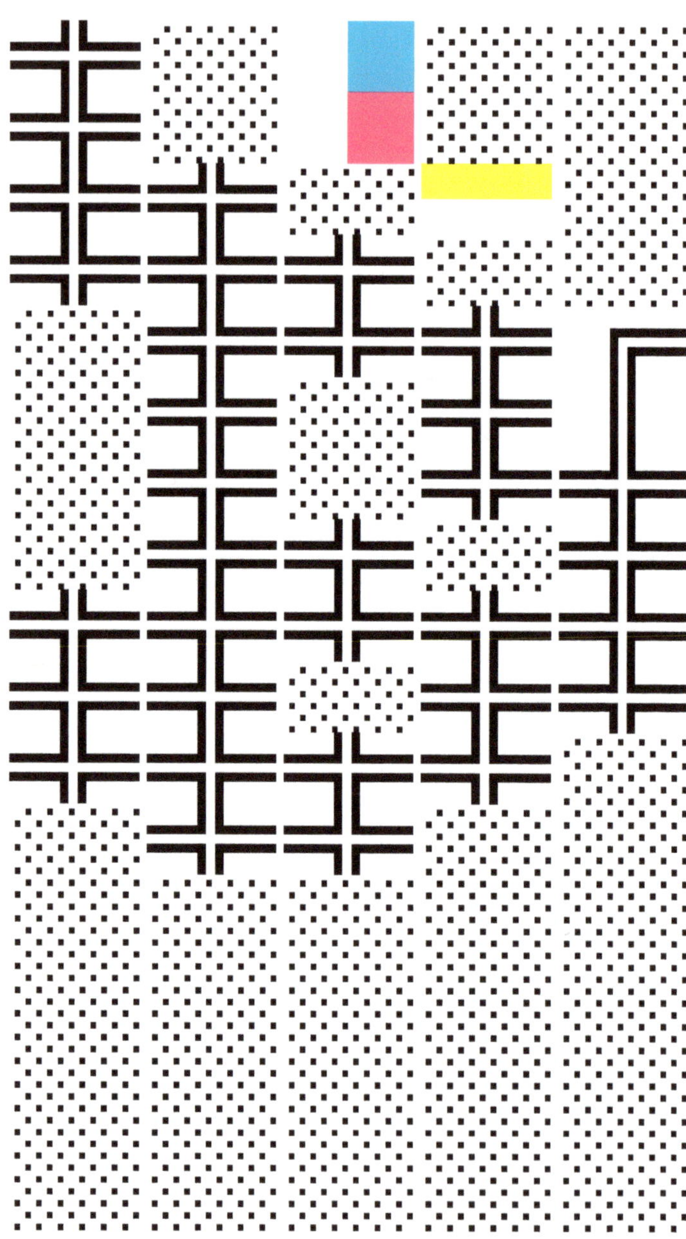

xli.

{
 predictable outcome
 / happiness
}

-

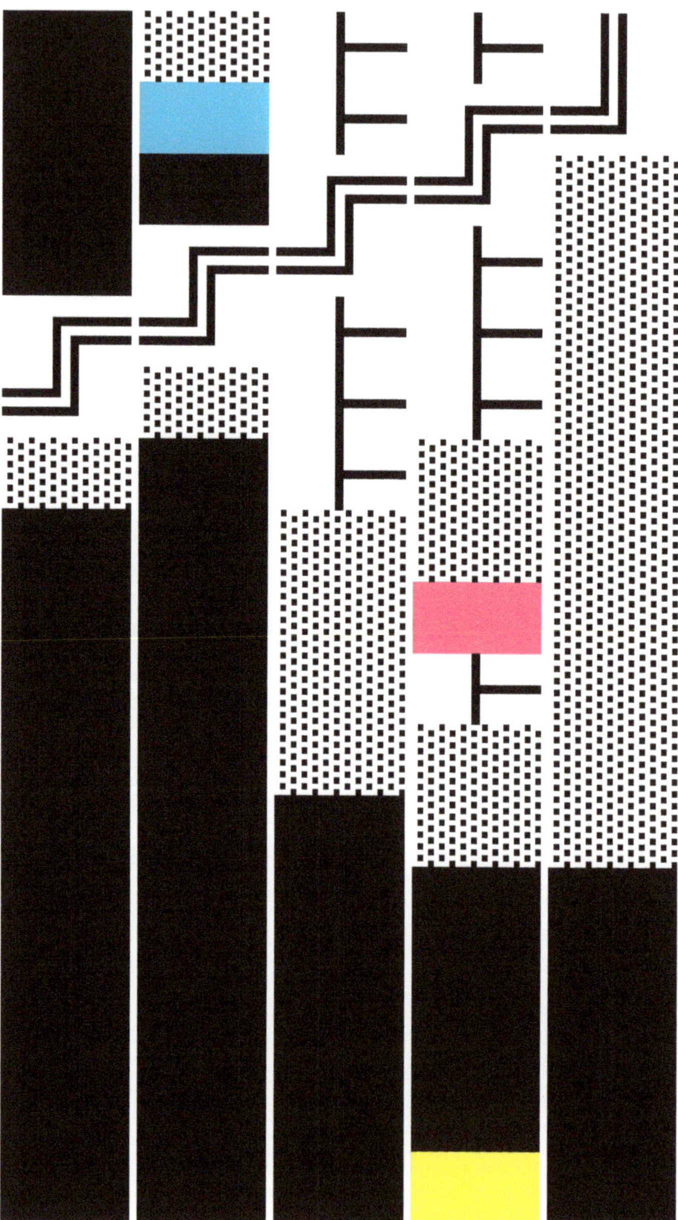

xlii.

{
 hardcore
     / myth
}

-

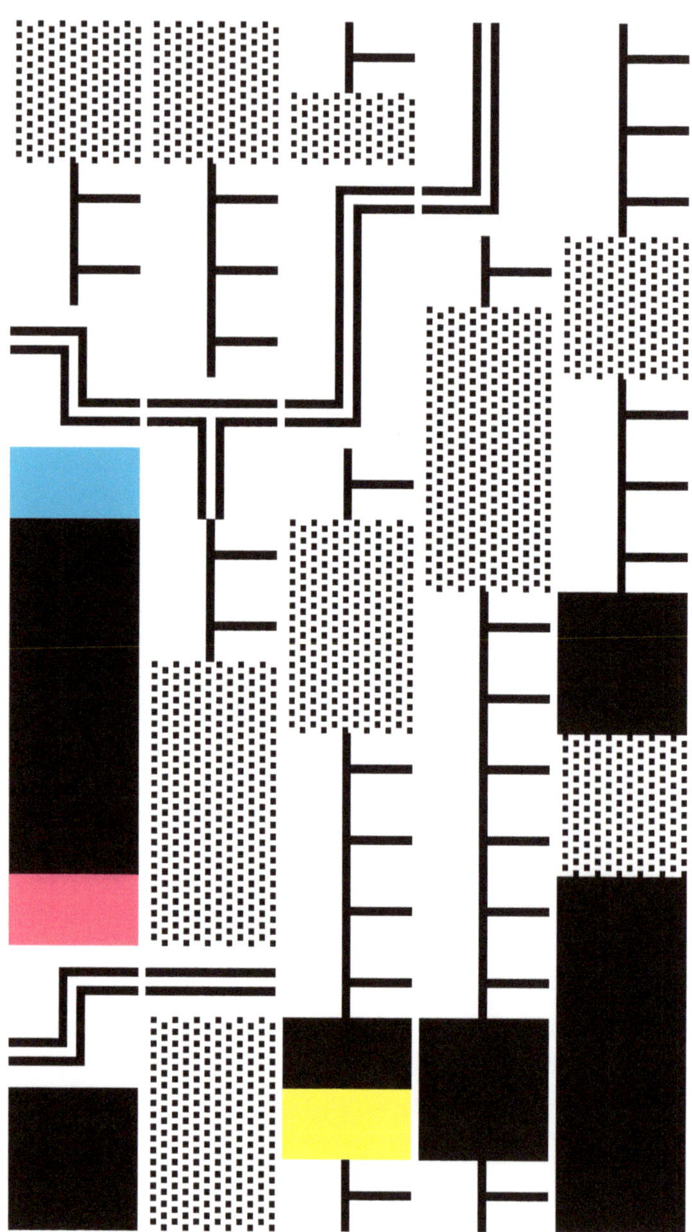

xliii.

{
 symbolic meaning
     / abstraction
}

-

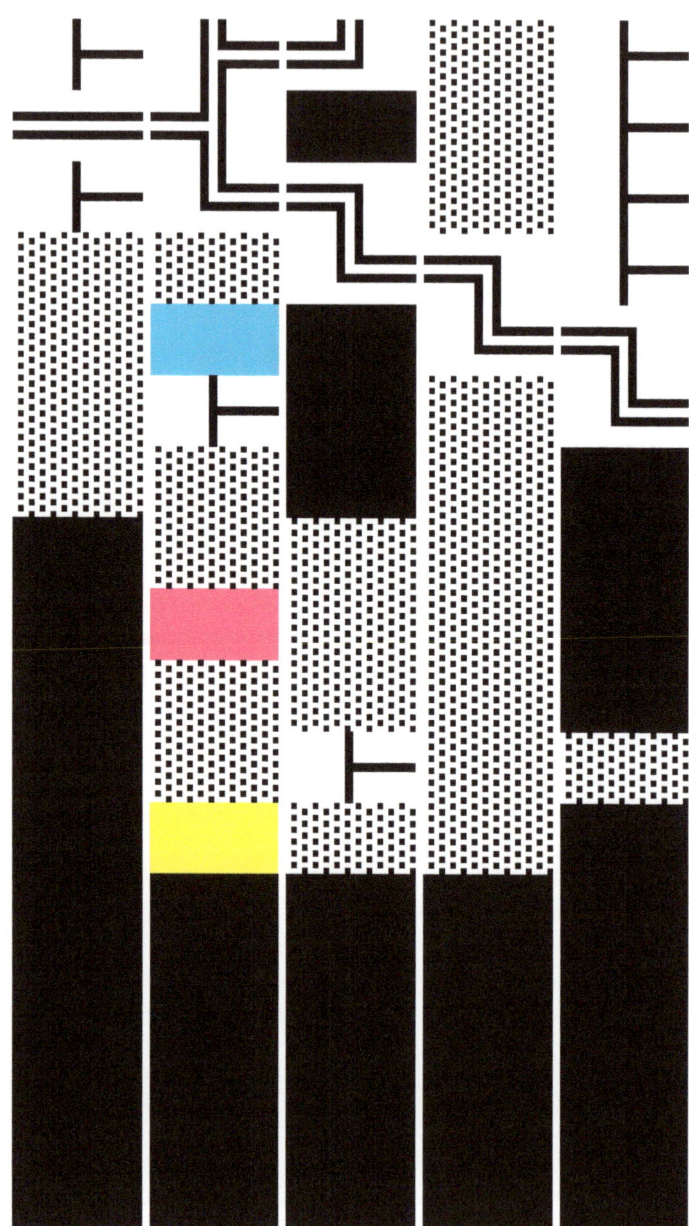

xliv.

{
 melancholy
     subtle form
          of joy
}

–

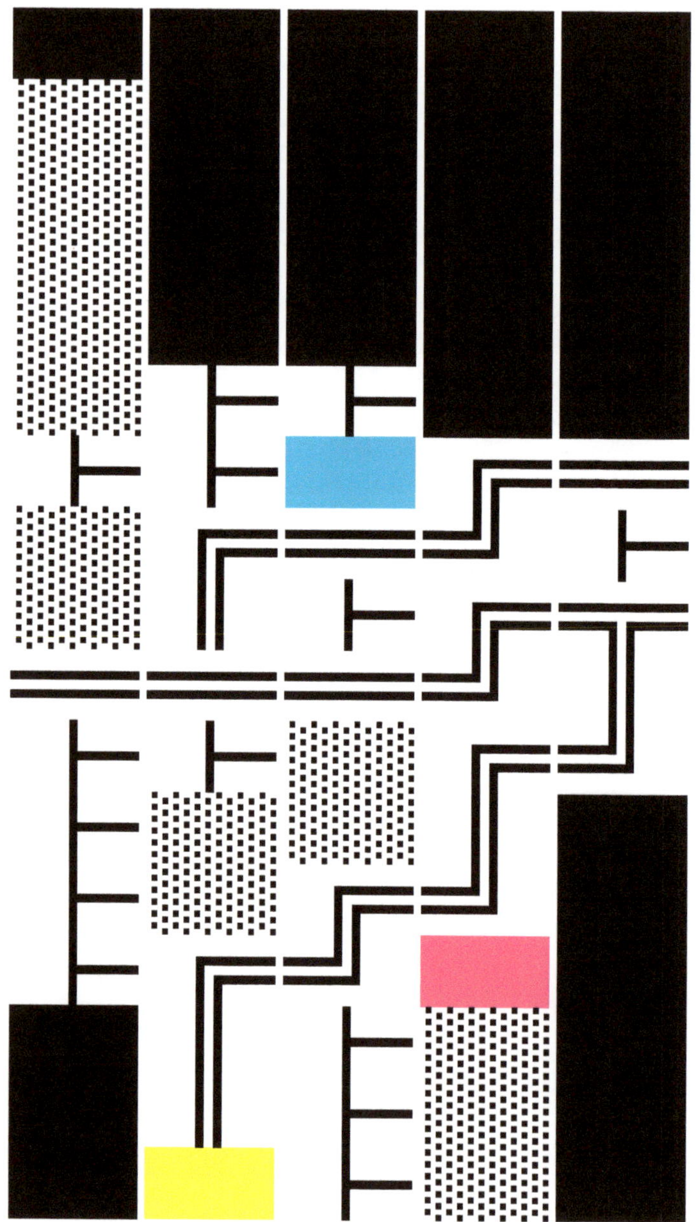

xlv.

{
 no fixed rules
     / only possibilities
}

-

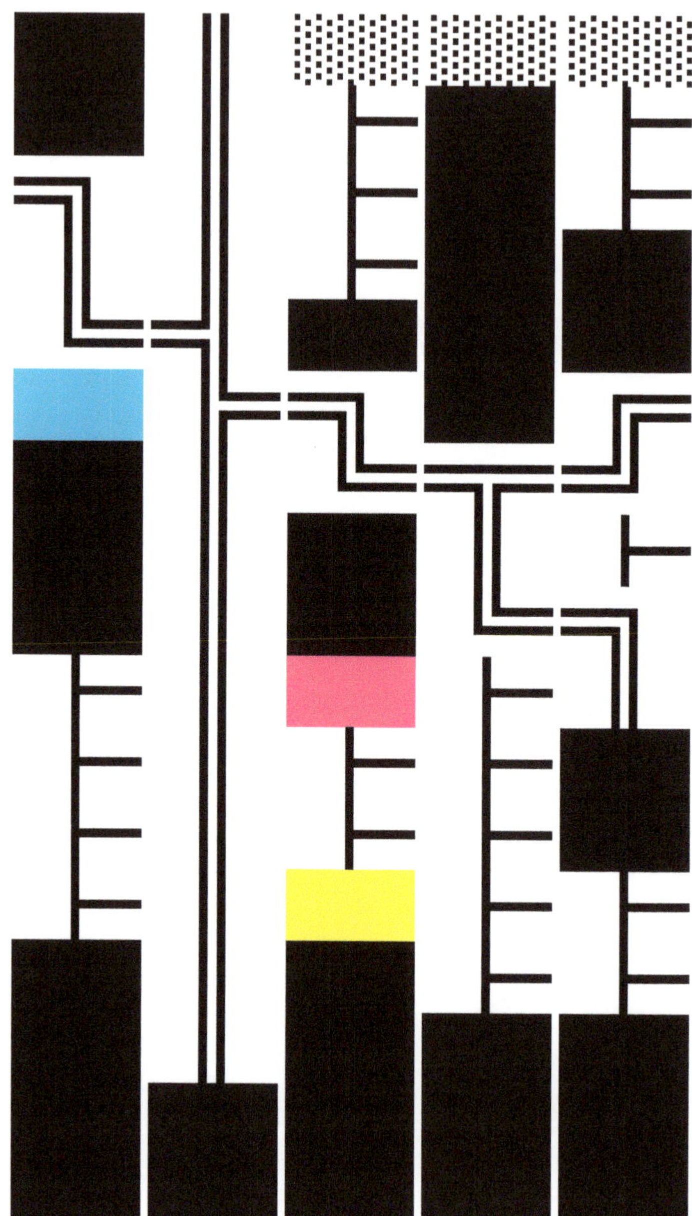

xlvi.

{
 every theory
     / fantastic
}

–

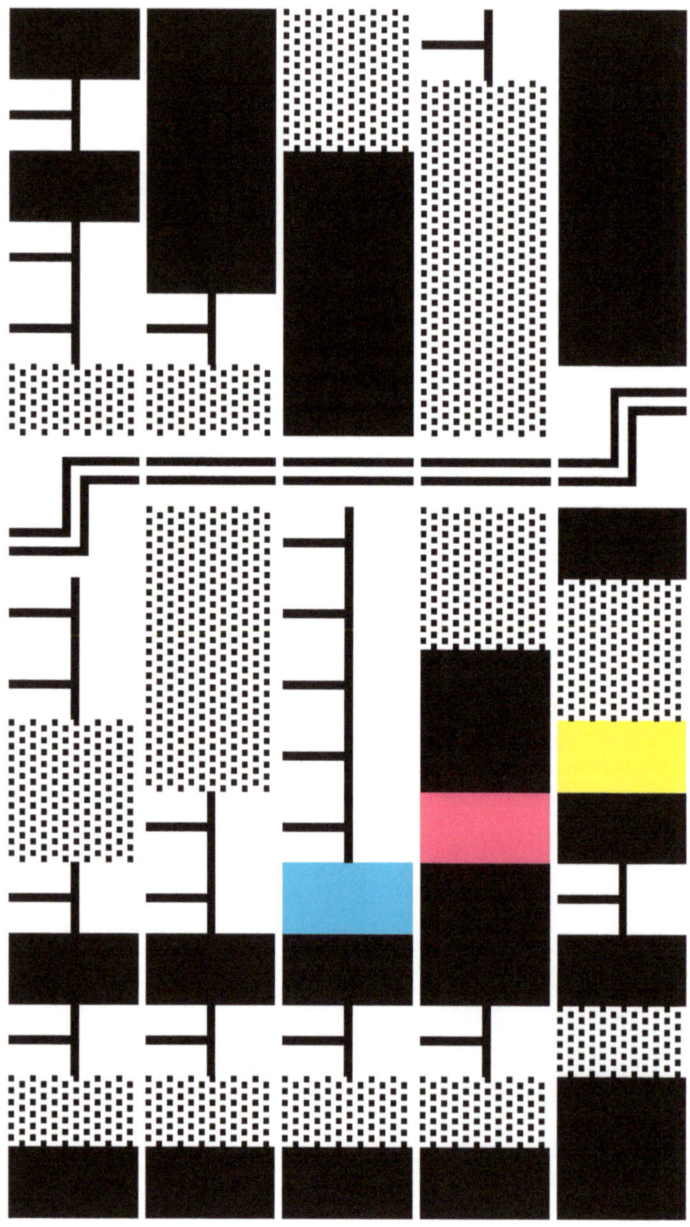

xlvii.

{<br>
 generalisations<br>
        / self-realising<br>
                  / prophecies<br>
}

-

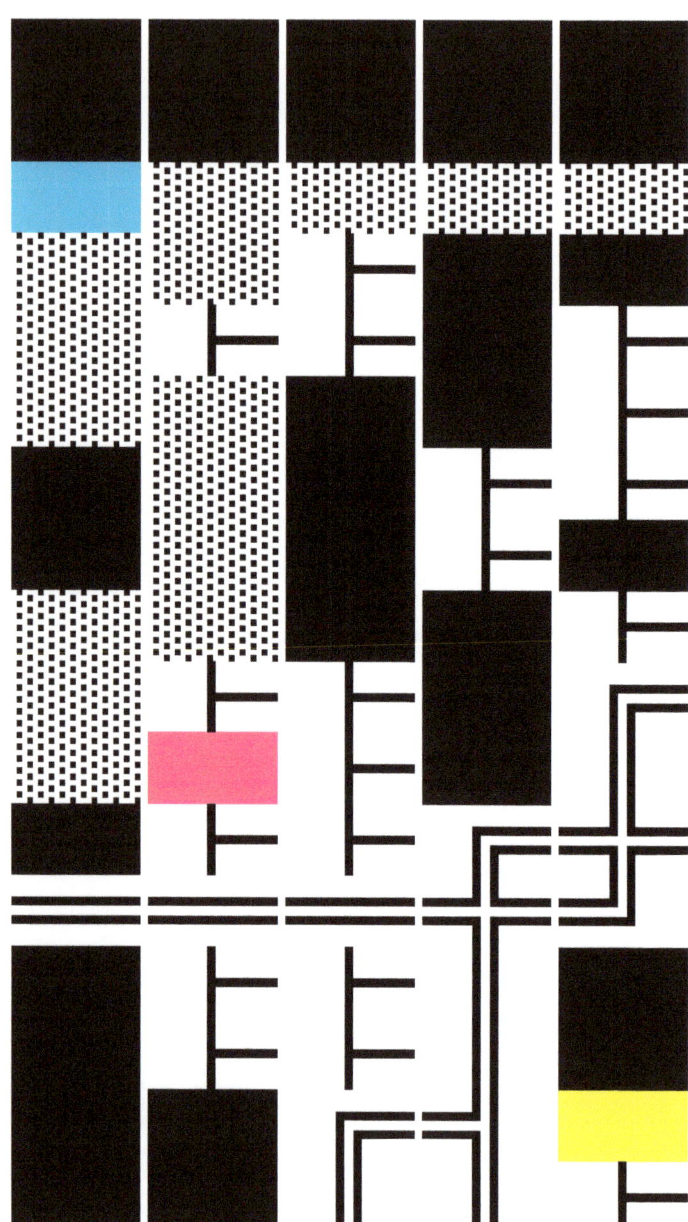

xlviii.

{
 ritual synthesis
     / material
     / spiritual
     / mental
}

-

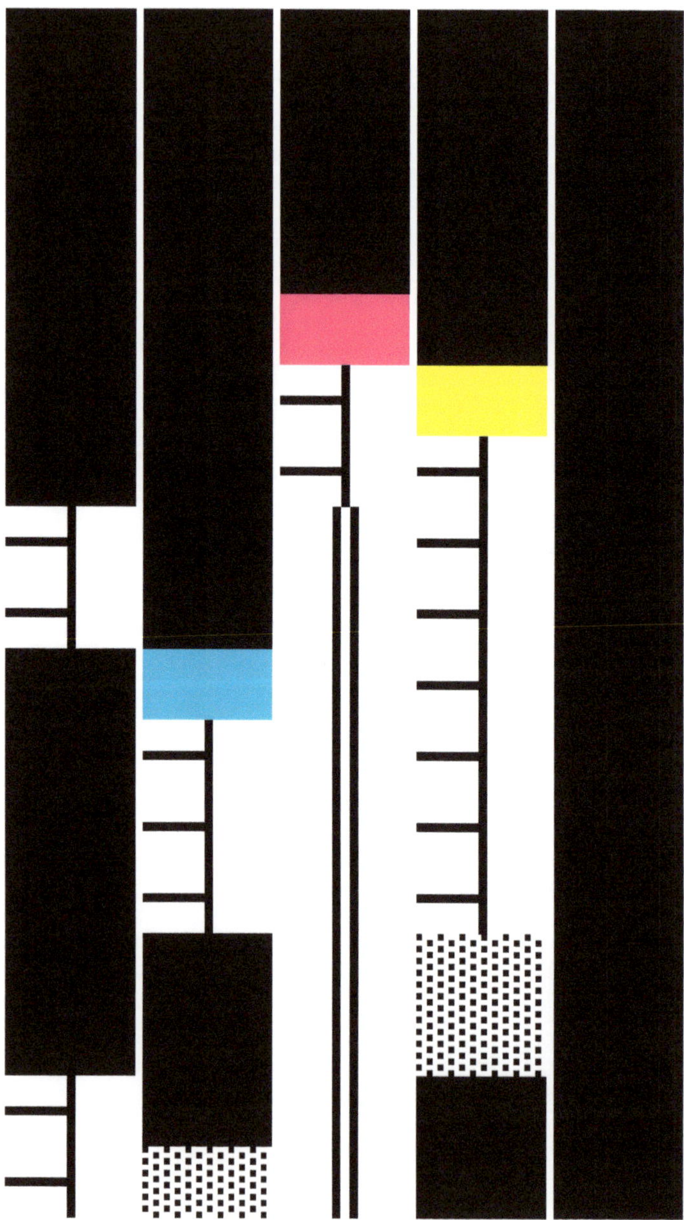

xlvix.

```
{
 maximum effect
      / minimum effort
}

-
```

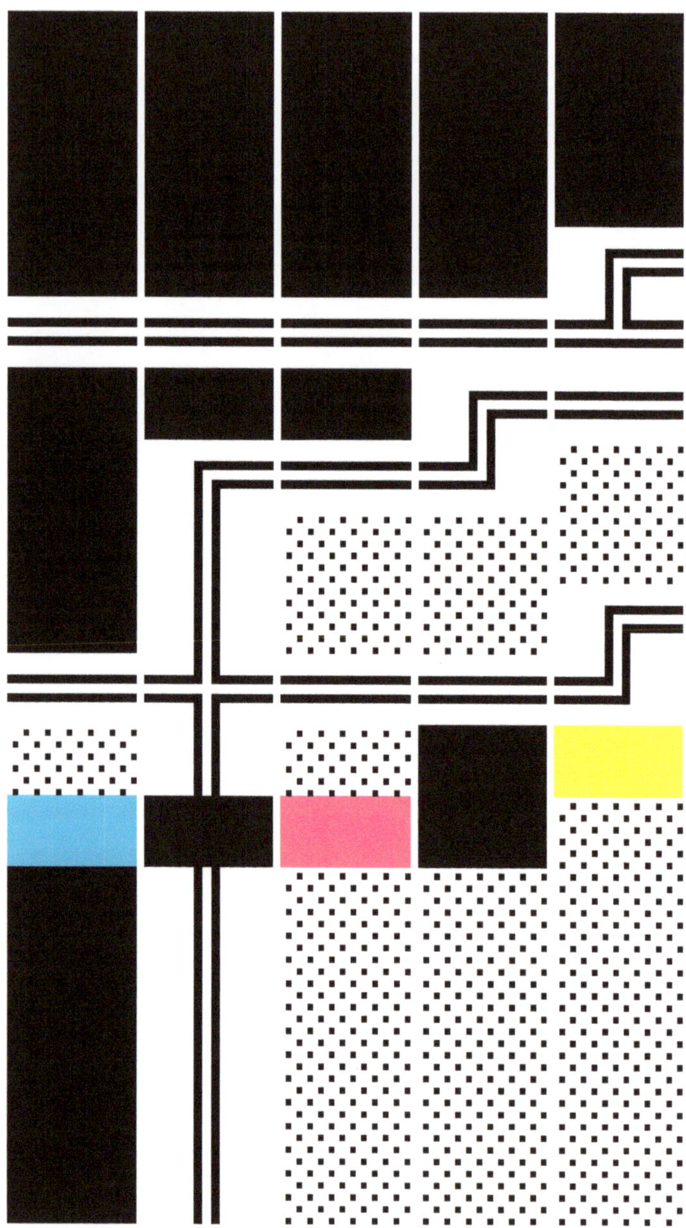

1.

{
consensus
/ off
}

-

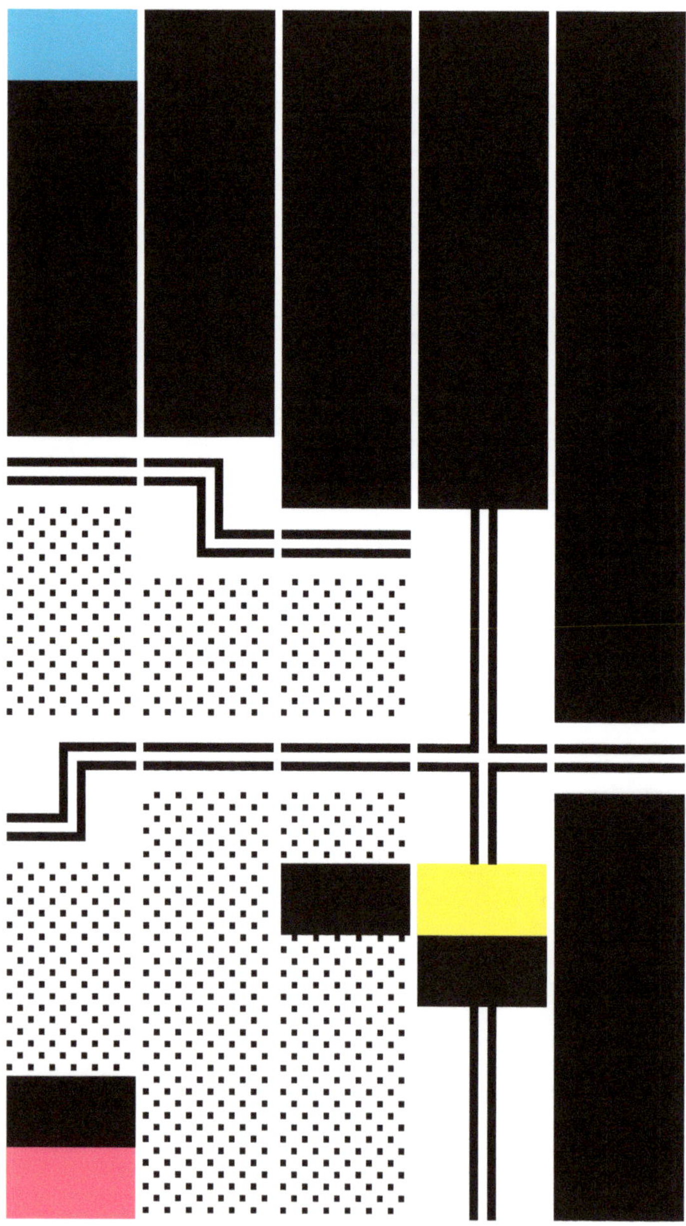

li.

{
 no more
     / than enough
}

-

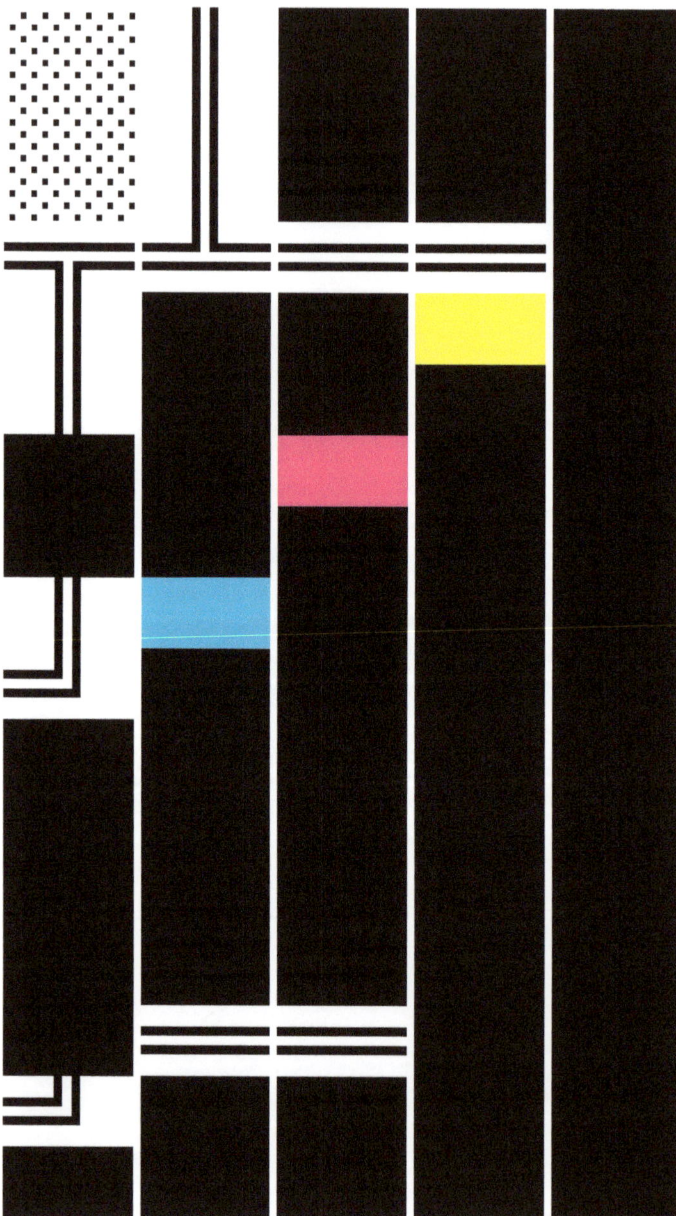

lii.

{
 cosmos
      / uncaring
}

–

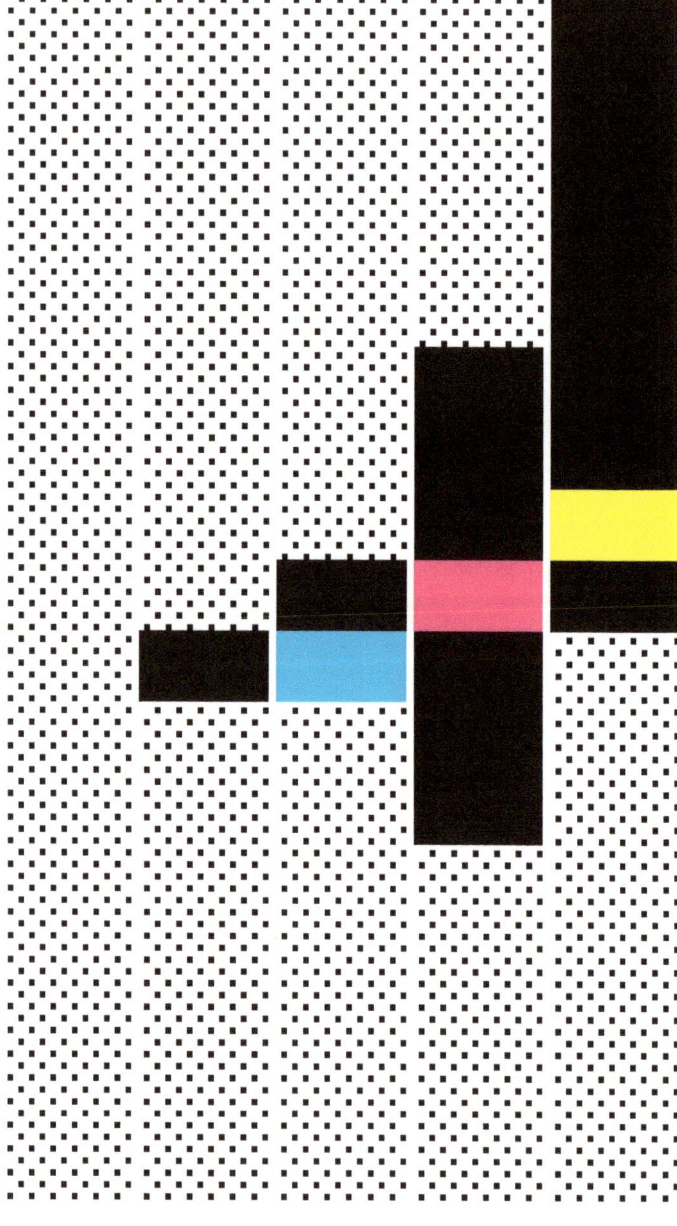

```
liii.

{
 form
     / ephemeral
 idea
     / perennial
}

-
```

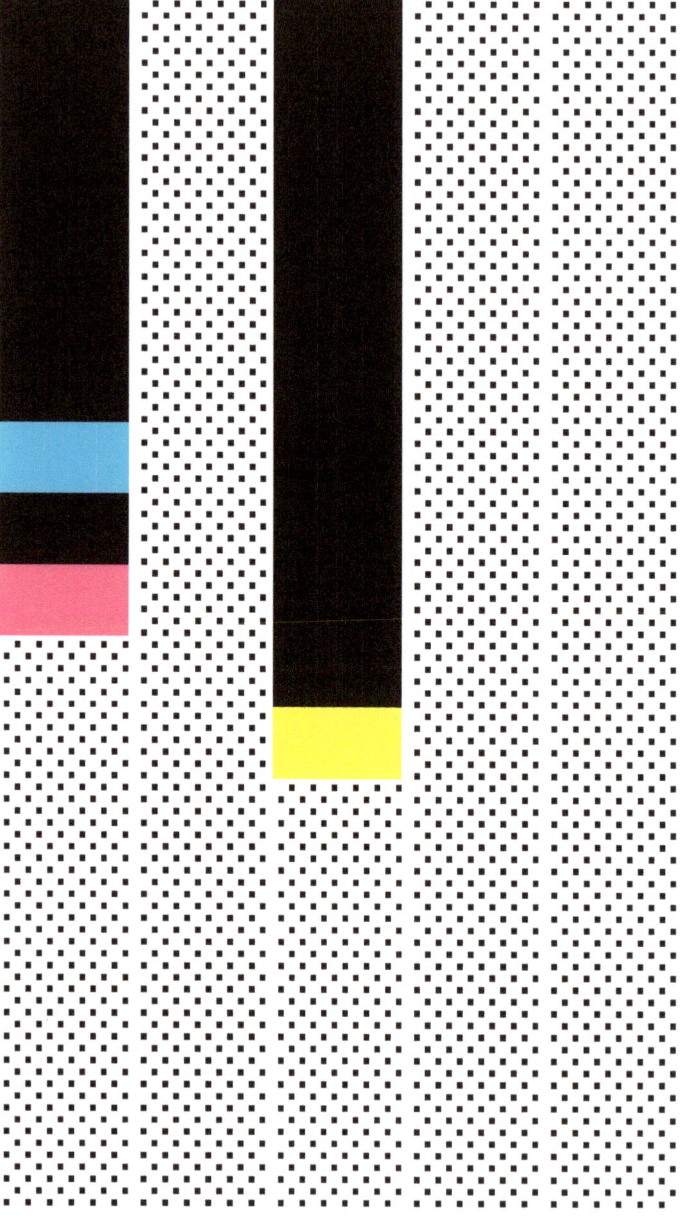

liv.

{
 fuelling life
     / death
}

–

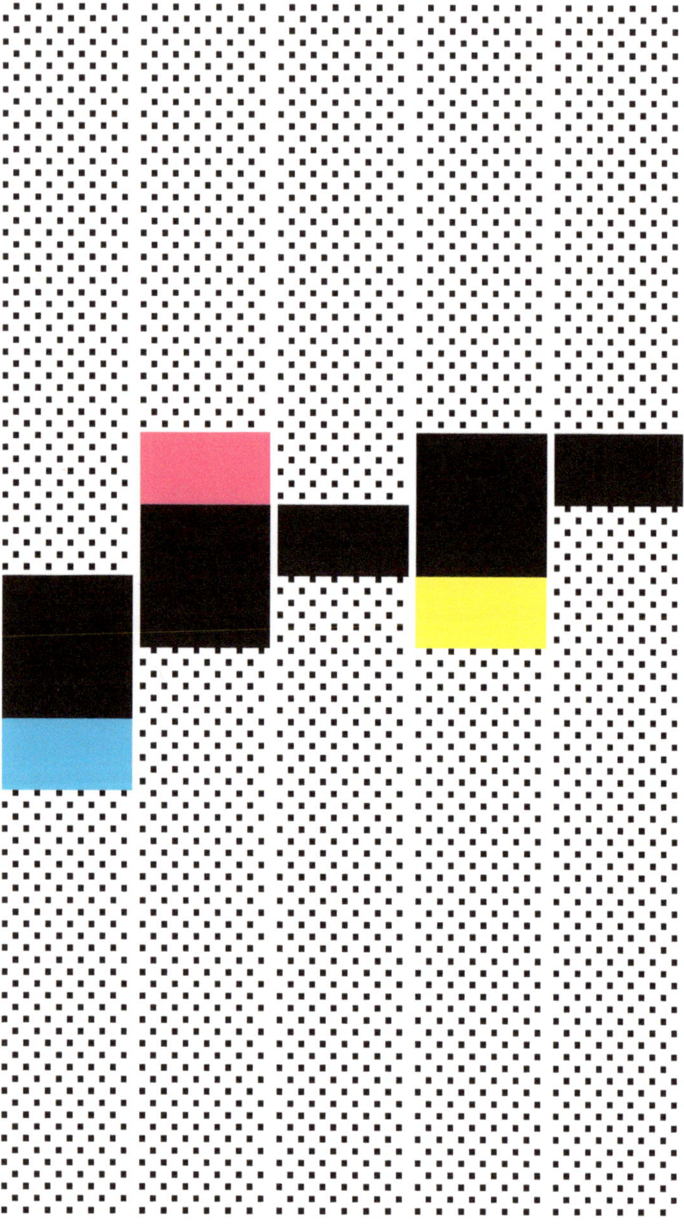

lv.

{
 no definitions
}

-

{
FUNDAMENTALISM
/
/ CH46R1N
/
/ set in inconsolata typeface

/ www.metafluxpublishing.com
}

–

www.ingramcontent.com/pod-product-compliance
Ingram Content Group UK Ltd.
Pitfield, Milton Keynes, MK11 3LW, UK
UKHW062306290726
14090UKWH00018B/916

9 780993 327247